Dear Adult Student,

Learning new things and building basic skills may be challenging for you, but they also can be very exciting. When you follow the guidelines for learning basic skills, you will be acquiring skills that will prepare you for life.

The skills that you will study and practice in this workbook will help you become more confident as you master them. These skills can help you with many things that you do in life, such as buying a car, shopping for groceries, applying for a job, reading maps, and recognizing signs.

You may be using this workbook on your own or as part of an adult education or training program that you are enrolled in. If this is your own copy, you may want to answer the practice questions right in the workbook or on the attached answer sheet in the back. If the workbook belongs to the classroom or program that you are enrolled in and will be used by other students, you should not write in it. Use a separate answer sheet instead.

Before you start your work, it would be helpful to find out which skills you need to work on. You may have taken a test such as TABE®—*Tests of Adult Basic Education.* These tests can be used to find out what skills you already know, and also to point out which skills need more work.

Once you have identified the skills you need to work on, go to the Table of Contents, find the section for one of the skills that you want to work on, turn to that page, and start doing the practice questions.

When you have finished the practice questions, you will find an answer key at the back of the workbook. You can use the answer key to check your work.

Best wishes for a successful and useful experience in using this workbook to get information and practice on the skills that you want to learn more about and would like to master. Congratulations on continuing your education.

Mastering the skills listed below can help you achieve your goals and improve many life skills, from reading the daily newspaper to getting a better job. Talk with your teacher about the skills that you need to work on. Find a skill section that you want to work on in the list below, turn to that section in your workbook, and start practicing.

The answers to the problems in each section are located in the Answer Key in the back of this workbook.

MULTIPLICATION OF WHOLE NUMBERS

Multiplication of whole numbers is the process of repeated addition to get a **product**. The multiplication problem $3 \times 2 = 6$ is the same as the addition problem $2 + 2 + 2 = 6$, or $3 + 3 = 6$.

Multiplication of Whole Numbers includes subskills, such as Basic Facts, No Regrouping, and Regrouping.

Look at these examples of multiplication of whole numbers. Choose your answer for each problem.

EXAMPLE	ANSWER

EXAMPLE

$$\begin{array}{r} 428 \\ \times\ 4 \\ \end{array}$$

a   1,682

b   1,692

c   1,712

d   1,704

e   None of these

ANSWER

- **Answer a is not** correct. No regrouping was done.

- **Answer b is not** correct. The 1 was carried into the tens column instead of the 3.

- **Answer c is** correct:

$$\begin{array}{r} {\scriptstyle 1\ 3} \\ 428 \\ \times\ 4 \\ \hline 1,712 \\ \end{array}$$

- **Answer d is not** correct. The incorrect multiplication fact $8 \times 4 = 24$ was used.

EXAMPLE	ANSWER

$45 \times 36 =$

a   1,620

b   1,590

c   1,660

d   1,520

e   None of these

- **Answer a is correct:**

$$
\begin{array}{r}
45 \\
\times\ 36 \\
\hline
270 \\
135 \\
\hline
1,620
\end{array}
$$

- **Answer b is not correct.** A three was not carried into the tens column.

- **Answer c is not correct.** The incorrect multiplication fact $6 \times 4 = 28$ was used.

- **Answer d is not correct.** The partial products were not added correctly.

Apply

Being able to multiply easily and quickly can simplify our lives. For example, you might want to know how many stamps are on a sheet that has 4 rows of 5 stamps. Multiply 4 times 5 instead of counting each stamp: $4 \times 5 = 20$.

Do these multiplication problems.
First, try Numbers 1 and 2 for practice.

1.   817
   $\times$ 6

    a   4,862

    b   4,902

    c   4,802

    d   4,962

    e   None of these

ANSWER *b* is correct: $6 \times 817 = 4,902$.

2. $7 \times 7,464 =$

    a   52,348

    b   52,328

    c   52,228

    d   53,248

    e   None of these

ANSWER *e* is correct. The correct answer, 52,248, is not given.

Now you are ready to do more problems. The answers to the
problems in this section can be found in the back of this workbook.

3. 747
    × 3

    a 2,141

    b 2,241

    c 2,121

    d 2,221

    e None of these

4. 186 × 9 =

    a 1,674

    b 1,774

    c 1,624

    d 1,724

    e None of these

When regrouping, it may be helpful to write the value of the number being regrouped above the place value to which it is being added.
For example:

Tip

$$\begin{array}{r} \overset{5}{2}8 \\ \times\ 7 \\ \hline 196 \end{array}$$

5.   68
       × 29

   a   1,902

   b   1,802

   c   1,972

   d   2,072

   e   None of these

6.   563
       × 28

   a   15,344

   b   15,664

   c   15,744

   d   15,764

   e   None of these

Tip

When multiplying numbers with two or more digits, line up the columns correctly.
For example:

$$
\begin{array}{r}
234 \\
\times\ \ 86 \\
\hline
1404 \\
1872\ \ \\
\hline
20{,}124 \\
\end{array}
$$

7. $94 \times 24 =$

   a 2,246

   b   376

   c   564

   d 2,256

   e None of these

8. $120 \times 260 =$

   a   3,020

   b   3,120

   c 30,200

   d 31,200

   e None of these

A multiplication problem such as $9 \times 3,588$ can be written in vertical format before multiplying:

$$\begin{array}{r} 3,588 \\ \times \quad 9 \\ \hline \end{array}$$

Reminder

For Numbers 9 through 12, write your answers.

9. $\begin{array}{r} 5,271 \\ \times\quad 3 \\ \hline \end{array}$

10. $350 \times 30 =$ _____

11. $470 \times 18 =$ _____

12. $\begin{array}{r} 507 \\ \times\ 176 \\ \hline \end{array}$

NOTES

DIVISION OF WHOLE NUMBERS

Division of whole numbers is a shortcut for the process of repeated subtraction in order to get a **quotient**. For example, 10 ÷ 2 means how many twos can be subtracted from 10, or how many groups of 2 are in 10.

10 − 2 = 8	
8 − 2 = 6	The 2 has been subtracted
6 − 2 = 4	5 times, or there are 5 groups
4 − 2 = 2	of 2 in 10. Therefore,
2 − 2 = 0	10 ÷ 2 = 5

Division of Whole Numbers includes subskills, such as No Remainder and Remainder.

Look at these examples of division of whole numbers. Choose your answer for each problem.

EXAMPLE	ANSWER
$15\overline{)750}$ a 5 b 30 c 50 d 53 e None of these	• **Answer a** is **not** correct. The division was not completed for the ones place. • **Answer b** is **not** correct. Fifteen goes into seventy-five 5 times, not 3 times. • **Answer c** is correct: $$\begin{array}{r} 50 \\ 15\overline{)750} \\ 75 \\ \hline 0 \end{array}$$ • **Answer d** is **not** correct. The 3 in the ones place should be a 0.

EXAMPLE	ANSWER

$746 \div 8 =$

a   93

b   93 R 2

c   83

d   83 R 2

e   None of these

- **Answer *a* is not** correct. The remainder was omitted.

- **Answer *b* is correct:**

$$\begin{array}{r} 93 \text{ R } 2 \\ 8\overline{)746} \\ \underline{72} \\ 26 \\ \underline{24} \\ 2 \end{array}$$

- **Answer *c* is not** correct. The tens place of the quotient is incorrect, and the remainder was omitted.

- **Answer *d* is not** correct. The tens place of the quotient is incorrect.

Apply

We may use division when we plan a meal for a group. Suppose six people want to share a 12-slice pizza equally. Divide 12 by 6 to determine how many slices of pizza each person should get: $12 \div 6 = 2$.

Do these division problems.
First, try Numbers 1 and 2 for practice.

1. $4\overline{)156}$

    a 34

    b 36

    c 37

    d 39

    e None of these

ANSWER *d* is correct: $4 \times 39 = 156$.

2. $13\overline{)481}$

    a 37

    b 39

    c 47

    d 49

    e None of these

ANSWER *a* is correct: $13 \times 37 = 481$.

Now you are ready to do more problems. The answers to the problems in this section can be found in the back of this workbook.

3. 814 ÷ 22 =

  a 27

  b 32

  c 42

  d 37

  e None of these

4. 153 ÷ 9 =

  a 17

  b 15 R 8

  c 18

  d 18 R 1

  e None of these

A division problem such as 252 ÷ 12 can be written as $12\overline{)252}$ before dividing.

5. 72 ÷ 6 =

   a 10 R 2

   b 11

   c 12

   d 13

   e None of these

6. 126 ÷ 7 =

   a 16 R 4

   b 16

   c 23 R 1

   d 18

   e None of these

7. $6\overline{)257}$

   a 39 R 5

   b 42 R 4

   c 49 R 2

   d 58 R 1

   e None of these

In the division problem $5\overline{)426}$, 5 is greater than 4, so divide 5 into 42 to get the first part of the answer (quotient).

Tip

8. 224 ÷ 14 =

  a 16 R 4

  b 18

  c 16

  d 12 R 8

  e None of these

9. 921 ÷ 6 =

  a 153 R 2

  b 135 R 3

  c 155 R 1

  d 153 R 1

  e None of these

In division, the remainder must always be less than the divisor.

Reminder

For Numbers 10 through 12, write your answers.

10. $368 \div 8 =$ _____

11. $608 \div 16 =$ _____

12. $9\overline{)385} =$ _____

NOTES

FRACTIONS

A *fraction* is a number that represents a part of a whole that has been divided into equal parts. An example of a fraction is one piece of a whole pie that has been cut into a number of equal-size pieces. Depending on the size of the pieces, you might get either $\frac{1}{4}$ or $\frac{1}{8}$ of the pie.

Fractions includes subskills, such as Addition, Subtraction, and Multiplication.

Look at these examples of fractions. Choose your answer for each problem.

EXAMPLE	ANSWER

$\frac{1}{6} + \frac{4}{6} =$

a $\frac{7}{10}$

b $\frac{5}{12}$

c   1

d $\frac{5}{6}$

e   None of these

- **Answer *a* is not correct.** The numerator and denominator of each fraction were added to form the numerator and denominator of the answer.

- **Answer *b* is not correct.** The numerators and denominators were added.

- **Answer *c* is not correct.** The numerators were added incorrectly.

- **Answer *d* is correct.** Since the fractions have the same denominator, that denominator remained the same in the answer. Only the numerators were added.

EXAMPLE	ANSWER

$7 - \frac{4}{5} =$

a $\frac{3}{5}$

b $6\frac{2}{5}$

c $6\frac{1}{5}$

d $7\frac{4}{5}$

e   None of these

- **Answer a** is **not** correct. The numerator of the fraction was subtracted from 7.

- **Answer b** is **not** correct. There was an error in computation.

- **Answer c** is correct. The 7 can be written as $6\frac{5}{5}$; therefore $6\frac{5}{5} - \frac{4}{5} = 6\frac{1}{5}$.

- **Answer d** is **not** correct. The numbers were added instead of subtracted.

Do these fraction problems.
First, try Numbers 1 and 2 for practice.

1. $\frac{1}{3} + \frac{5}{8} =$

  a $\frac{6}{11}$

  b $\frac{13}{24}$

  c $\frac{7}{24}$

  d $\frac{2}{3}$

  e None of these

ANSWER **e** is correct. The fractions should be written with a common denominator, then added: $\frac{1}{3} + \frac{5}{8} = \frac{8}{24} + \frac{15}{24} = \frac{23}{24}$. The correct answer, $\frac{23}{24}$, is not given.

2. $\begin{array}{r} 2\frac{2}{8} \\ + 3\frac{3}{8} \\ \hline \end{array}$

  a $6\frac{1}{4}$

  b $5\frac{5}{8}$

  c $6\frac{7}{8}$

  d $5\frac{7}{16}$

  e None of these

ANSWER **b** is correct.

Now you are ready to do more problems. The answers to the problems in this section can be found in the back of this workbook.

3.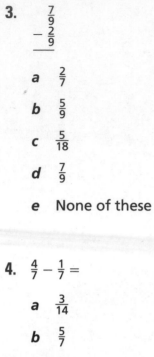

- **a** $\frac{2}{7}$
- **b** $\frac{5}{9}$
- **c** $\frac{5}{18}$
- **d** $\frac{7}{9}$
- **e** None of these

4. $\frac{4}{7} - \frac{1}{7} =$

- **a** $\frac{3}{14}$
- **b** $\frac{5}{7}$
- **c** $\frac{3}{7}$
- **d** $\frac{5}{14}$
- **e** None of these

Fractions are often used in recipes ($\frac{1}{2}$ cup sugar), in measurements ($5\frac{1}{4}$ inches of ribbon, $\frac{3}{4}$ pound of potatoes), and in observations (the stadium is $\frac{1}{2}$ full).

5. $2 \times \frac{1}{8} =$

   a $\frac{1}{4}$

   b $\frac{1}{16}$

   c $\frac{1}{2}$

   d $\frac{1}{8}$

   e None of these

6. $\frac{3}{4} \times \frac{2}{9} =$

   a $\frac{1}{36}$

   b $\frac{1}{12}$

   c $\frac{1}{6}$

   d $\frac{1}{3}$

   e None of these

Reminder

Multiplication of fractions may be simplified by reducing before multiplying. Reducing is dividing by a common factor. Divide the common factor into any numerator *and* any denominator. Then multiply the numerators and multiply the denominators. For example:

$$\frac{\overset{1}{\cancel{3}}}{\underset{2}{\cancel{8}}} \times \frac{\overset{1}{\cancel{4}}}{\underset{5}{\cancel{15}}} = \frac{1}{2} \times \frac{1}{5} = \frac{1}{10}$$

7. $\frac{2}{7} \div \frac{3}{7} =$

    a $\frac{6}{49}$

    b $1\frac{1}{2}$

    c $\frac{6}{7}$

    d $\frac{2}{3}$

    e   None of these

8. $\frac{5}{6} \div \frac{11}{12} =$

    a $\frac{10}{11}$

    b $\frac{11}{10}$

    c $\frac{5}{22}$

    d $\frac{5}{11}$

    e   None of these

To divide fractions, invert the second fraction (the divisor), then follow the rules for multiplying fractions.
For example:

$$\frac{1}{3} \div \frac{4}{5} = \frac{1}{3} \times \frac{5}{4} = \frac{5}{12}$$

For Numbers 9 through 12, write your answers.

9. $7\frac{9}{10} + \frac{4}{5} =$ _____

10. $\frac{13}{16} - \frac{3}{8} =$ _____

11. $\frac{2}{3} \times \frac{1}{2} =$ _____

12. $\frac{2}{5} \div \frac{1}{2} =$ _____

Reminder

The value of a fraction is unchanged if the numerator and denominator are multiplied (or divided) by the same number. The reason the value is unchanged is that the fraction is being multiplied (or divided) by 1. For example:

$$\frac{3}{5} \times \frac{4}{4} = \frac{12}{20} \quad \text{or} \quad \frac{15 \div 3}{18 \div 3} = \frac{5}{6}$$

NOTES

DECIMALS

A *decimal* number is a number that contains a decimal point. The decimal point separates the whole number from its fractional part. The digits to the right of the decimal point represent the fractional part of the whole number.

A decimal point is used when representing money. The digits to the right of the decimal point represent the fractional part (cents) of one dollar.

Decimals includes subskills, such as Addition and Subtraction with No Regrouping and Regrouping.

Look at these examples of decimals. Choose your answer for each problem.

EXAMPLE	ANSWER
$0.3 + 0.3 =$ a 0.06 b 6.0 c 0.006 d 0.6 e None of these	• **Answer a** is **not** correct. The numbers were added in the hundredths place instead of the tenths place. • **Answer b** is **not** correct. The numbers were added in the tens place instead of the tenths place. • **Answer c** is **not** correct. The numbers were added in the thousandths place instead of the tenths place. • **Answer d** is correct. Three tenths plus three tenths equals six tenths.

EXAMPLE	ANSWER

$195 \div 2.5 =$

a   7.8

b 78.25

c   0.78

d 78

e None of these

- **Answer a** is **not** correct. The decimal point was incorrectly placed.

- **Answer b** is **not** correct. There was an error in computation.

- **Answer c** is **not** correct. The decimal point was incorrectly placed.

- **Answer d** is correct:

$$
\begin{array}{r}
7\,8. \\
2.5\overline{)195.0.} \\
175 \\
\hline
200 \\
200 \\
\hline
0
\end{array}
$$

Do these decimal problems.
First, try Numbers 1 and 2 for practice.

1. $4.05 + $0.08 =

    a $4.03

    b $4.85

    c $4.58

    d $4.40

    e   None of these

ANSWER *e* is correct. The correct answer, $4.13, is not given.

2. $85.15 − $36.72 =

    a $49.43

    b $48.87

    c $48.43

    d $48.33

    e   None of these

ANSWER *c* is correct: $85.15 − $36.72 = $48.43.

Now you are ready to do more problems. The answers to the problems in this section can be found in the back of this workbook.

3. $73.05 + 6.34 =$

   a 79.49

   b 73.69

   c 79.39

   d 79.65

   e None of these

4.
$$\begin{array}{r} 73.301 \\ -\ 54.729 \end{array}$$

   a 28.682

   b 18.572

   c 18.672

   d 28.582

   e None of these

Every time a price is listed in dollars and cents (such as $3.65), a decimal is used. A decimal is another way to represent part of a whole, such as 12.93 gallons of gasoline or 1.5 pounds of ground beef.

Weight: 1.5 lbs.
COST: $3.65

5. 92.3 × 8.2 =

a 756.86

b 7,568.6

c 738.86

d 7,388.6

e None of these

6. 631.54
  × 7

a 442.078

b 4,420.78

c 442,078.0

d 44.2078

e None of these

Tip

When multiplying decimals, add the number of decimal places in the two factors. That will tell you how many decimal places should be in the answer. For example:

0.027	3 decimal places
× 0.06	+ 2 decimal places
0.00162	5 decimal places

7. $\dfrac{1{,}539}{2.7} =$

    a   570

    b   57

    c   5,700

    d   5.7

    e   None of these

8. $15\overline{)3.45}$

    a   0.23

    b   0.023

    c   2.3

    d   23.0

    e   None of these

When dividing by a decimal, move the decimal point in the divisor all the way to the right. Then move the decimal point in the dividend the same number of places. In the example below, the decimal points are moved by multiplying by the number 1, written in the form of $\frac{100}{100}$.

$$.25\overline{)1.97.5}$$

For Numbers 9 through 12, write your answers.

9. $3.87 + $9.78 = _____

10.   11.112
  − 10.021
        ‾‾‾‾‾‾‾

11.   0.507 × 1.4 = _____

12.   38.4 ÷ 0.24 = _____

NOTES

INTEGERS

The set of numbers called *integers* is the set of whole numbers and their opposites. Numbers such as 16, $^-40$, and 0 are all integers. But fractions such as $\frac{1}{2}$ and decimals such as $^-4.5$ are not integers.

Integers includes subskills, such as Addition, Subtraction, Multiplication, and Division.

Look at these examples of integers. Choose your answer for each problem.

EXAMPLE	ANSWER
$^-4 + (^-2) =$ a $\quad ^-6$ b $\quad ^-2$ c $\quad 8$ d $\quad 2$ e $\quad$ None of these	• **Answer a** is correct. Both $^-4$ and $^-2$ are negative, and $4 + 2 = 6$, so the answer is $^-6$. • **Answer b** is **not** correct. This would be the answer to $^-4 + 2$. • **Answer c** is **not** correct. The numbers $^-4$ and $^-2$ were multiplied instead of added. • **Answer d** is **not** correct. This would be the answer to $4 + (^-2)$.

EXAMPLE	ANSWER

$^-18 \div (^-6) =$

a $^-12$

b 3

c $^-3$

d 108

e None of these

- **Answer *a*** is **not** correct. Subtraction was performed instead of division.

- **Answer *b*** is correct. A negative number divided by a negative number gives a positive answer.

- **Answer *c*** is **not** correct. The answer should be positive, not negative.

- **Answer *d*** is **not** correct. The numbers were multiplied instead of divided.

Do these integer problems.
First, try Numbers 1 and 2 for practice.

1. $17 + (^-13) =$

a   30

b $^-4$

c $^-30$

d   4

e   None of these

ANSWER *d* is correct. If you locate 17 on a number line, then add $^-13$ by moving 13 places to the left, the answer is 4.

2. $4 + 1 + (^-10) =$

a $^-5$

b   13

c   5

d $^-13$

e   None of these

ANSWER *a* is correct: $4 + 1 + (^-10) = 5 + (^-10) = ^-5$.

Now you are ready to do more problems. The answers to the problems in this section can be found in the back of this workbook.

Negative integers are used when temperatures drop below zero. When the temperature is ⁻10°F, it's very cold. Negative integers also can be used to describe descending objects. A depth of ⁻75 feet means "75 feet below sea level."

3. ⁻13 − 12 =

 a   ⁻1

 b   ⁻25

 c   1

 d   25

 e   None of these

To subtract integers, add the opposite of the subtrahend. Then solve as addition of integers. For example:

$$5 - (^-10) = 5 + (10) = 15$$
or
$$^-6 - 9 = {}^-6 + {}^-9 = {}^-15$$

4. 3 − (⁻8) =

    a   5

    b   ⁻5

    c   11

    d   ⁻11

    e   None of these

5. ⁻100 × 4 =

    a   400

    b   ⁻400

    c   4,000

    d   ⁻40

    e   None of these

Reminder

When multiplying or dividing integers, if the signs are the same, the result is positive. If the signs are different, the result is negative.

6. $^-6 \times (^-9) =$

   a   54

   b   15

   c $^-15$

   d $^-54$

   e   None of these

7. $^-55 \div {}^-5 =$

   a $^-10$

   b $^-11$

   c   10

   d   11

   e   None of these

8. $36 \div {}^-9 =$

   a $^-27$

   b $^-4$

   c   27

   d   4

   e   None of these

For Numbers 9 through 12, write your answers.

9. $9 + (^-10) + (^-8) = $ _____

10. $16 - (^-4) = $ _____

11. $^-7 \times 2 \times 3 = $ _____

12. $^-69 \div 3 = $ _____

NOTES

PERCENTS

The *percent* symbol (%) comes from the number 100. Think of placing the "1" between the zeros, slanting it, and making it longer. You can say the percent symbol means "divide by 100." Therefore, $1\% = \frac{1}{100}$ and $50\% = \frac{50}{100}$, which also can be reduced to $\frac{1}{2}$.

Percents includes subskills, such as Percents.

Look at these examples of percents. Choose your answer for each problem.

EXAMPLE	ANSWER
1% of 90 =	• **Answer *a*** is **not** correct. This is 100% of 90.
a 90.0	• **Answer *b*** is **not** correct. The number 1 was subtracted from 90.
b 89.0	
c 9.0	• **Answer *c*** is **not** correct. This is 10% of 90.
d 0.9	
e None of these	• **Answer *d*** is correct. To find 1% of 90, first change 1% to a fraction: $1\% = \frac{1}{100}$. Then multiply: $\frac{1}{100} \times 90 = \frac{90}{100} = \frac{9}{10} = 0.9$.

EXAMPLE	ANSWER
What percent of 150 is 30? *a* 2% *b* 20% *c* 5% *d* 0.2% *e* None of these	• **Answer *a*** is **not** correct. The correct division problem ($30 \div 150 = 0.2$) was done, but 0.2 is not equal to 2%. • **Answer *b*** is correct. The first step is to divide 30 by 150. The answer, 0.2, equals 20%. • **Answer *c*** is **not** correct. The division of 150 by 30 was performed instead of dividing 30 by 150. • **Answer *d*** is **not** correct. The decimal 0.2 was not correctly changed into a percent.

You might use percents to calculate a 25% discount, a 6% sales tax, or a 15% tip.

Do these problems with percents.
First, try Numbers 1 and 2 for practice.

1. 25% of 80 =

   a   200.0

   b   2.0

   c   0.2

   d   20.0

   e   None of these

   ANSWER *d* is correct. 25% can be converted to the decimal 0.25, then multiplied by 80: $0.25 \times 80 = 20$.

2. 2% of 300 =

   a   6

   b   15

   c   60

   d   150

   e   None of these

   ANSWER *a* is correct. 2% can be converted to the decimal 0.02, then multiplied by 300: $0.02 \times 300 = 6$.

Now you are ready to do more problems. The answers to the problems in this section can be found in the back of this workbook.

3. 30% of 90 =

   a   2.7

   b   3.0

   c   27

   d   30

   e   None of these

To find a percentage of an amount, change the percent to a decimal by moving the decimal point two places to the left and dropping the percent symbol. Then multiply. For example:

$$12\% \text{ of } 40 = 0.12 \times 40 = 4.8$$

4. What percent of 100 is 40?

   a   0.4%

   b   4%

   c   40%

   d   400%

   e   None of these

5. What percent of 400 is 20?

   a   5%

   b   50%

   c   2%

   d   20%

   e   None of these

To solve a problem such as "35% of ☐ = 140" or "What percent of 15 is 12?", always take the number next to the word "of" and divide it into the number that follows the word "is" or follows the " = " sign. For example:

    1) 35% of ☐ = 140   2) What percent of 15 is 12?

      $\frac{140}{0.35} = 400$ $\frac{12}{15} = 0.8 = 80\%$

6. What percent of 10 is 7?

    a   0.7%

    b   7%

    c   70%

    d 700%

    e None of these

7. 10% of ☐ = 50

    a   2

    b   5

    c   200

    d 5,000

    e None of these

To change a number from decimal form to percent form, move the decimal point two places to the right and attach the percent symbol. For example:

$$0.23 = 23\% \quad 0.6 = 0.60 = 60\%$$
$$0.08 = 8\% \quad\quad 7 = 7.00 = 700\%$$

8. 50% of ☐ = 2

   a   1

   b   4

   c   10

   d   25

   e   None of these

9. 15% of ☐ = 9

   a   1.35

   b   13.5

   c   60

   d   600

   e   None of these

Reminder

To convert a percent to a fraction, write the percent as a fraction with a denominator of 100. Reduce the fraction, if possible. For example:

$$40\% = \frac{40}{100} = \frac{2}{5}$$

For Numbers 10 through 12, write your answers.

10. 20% of ☐ = 12 _____

11. What percent of 32 is 8? _____

12. 5% of 60 = _____

NUMBER AND NUMBER OPERATIONS

Number and number operations involves understanding the properties of a number system, and how numbers in the system may be represented and used.

Number and Number Operations includes subskills, such as Compare, Order, Fractional Part, Percent, Ratio, and Proportion.

Look at these examples of number and number operations. Choose your answer for each problem.

EXAMPLE	ANSWER
Which of these decimals is the equivalent of $\frac{5}{8}$? a 0.58 b 0.620 c 0.625 d 1.6	• **Answer a** is **not** correct. The numerator and denominator of the fraction have simply been used as the digits in a decimal number. • **Answer b** is **not** correct. The division problem 5 ÷ 8 was not completed correctly. • **Answer c** is correct. When 5 is divided by 8, the result is 0.625. • **Answer d** is **not** correct. This is the decimal equivalent of $\frac{8}{5}$ instead of $\frac{5}{8}$.

EXAMPLE	ANSWER
A small company has 8 full-time employees and 4 part-time employees. What is the ratio of full-time to part-time employees?	• **Answer a** is **not** correct. This is the ratio of part-time to full-time employees.
a 1:2	• **Answer b** is correct. The ratio of full-time to part-time employees is 8:4, which is the same as 2:1.
b 2:1	• **Answer c** is **not** correct. This is the ratio of the number of part-time employees to the total number of employees.
c 1:3	
d 3:1	• **Answer d** is **not** correct. This is the ratio of the total number of employees to the number of part-time employees.

If you see the same jacket priced at $39.59 at one store and $37.99 at another store, you use number and number operations to compare the prices. You also use number and number operations when you read an amount such as $\frac{3}{4}$ teaspoon in a recipe, or notice that it took 11.36 gallons of gasoline to fill your car's gas tank.

Do these number and number operations problems. First, try Numbers 1 and 2 for practice.

1. Which of these numbers is ninety-five thousand, eighty-six?

    a   90,586

    b   95,086

    c   905,086

    d 9,500,086

    ANSWER *b* is correct. The number 95,086 means 9 ten thousands, 5 thousands, 0 hundreds, 8 tens, and 6 ones.

2. The regular price of a telephone is $48. If the telephone is on sale for $\frac{1}{4}$ off, what is the sale price?

    a $12

    b $24

    c $36

    d $44

    ANSWER *c* is correct. To find $\frac{1}{4}$ of 48, you can multiply: $\frac{1}{4} \times 48 = 12$. The discount is $12, and the sale price is $48 − $12 = $36.

Now you are ready to do more problems. The answers to the problems in this section can be found in the back of this workbook.

3. Which of these numbers is eight hundred two million, sixty-four thousand, three hundred five?

  a   80,264,305

  b   800,264,305

  c   802,064,305

  d 8,002,640,305

4. Which of these is the same as the expression shown in the box below?

20,000,000 + 2,000,000 + 100,000 + 5,000 + 700

  a 22,100,700

  b 22,105,700

  c 22,150,700

  d 22,157,000

To understand large numbers, you must understand place value. For instance, the number 35,207 equals 3 ten thousands + 5 thousands + 2 hundreds + 7 ones.

Reminder

The table below shows the sales tax rate in five different counties. Study the table. Then do Numbers 5 through 7.

Sales Tax Rates

County	Tax Rate
P	5%
Q	7.25%
R	6.75%
S	6.25%
T	7%

5. Which of these tax rates is greater than the rate in County R but less than the rate in County T?

    a 6.5%

    b 7.1%

    c 6.7%

    d 6.9%

Reminder

The percent sign (%) means "per hundred" or "divided by 100." For example:

$$23\% = \frac{23}{100} \qquad 7\% = \frac{7}{100}$$

$$\frac{1}{2}\% = \frac{\frac{1}{2}}{100} = \frac{1}{200} \qquad 3.5\% = \frac{3.5}{100} = \frac{35}{1000} = \frac{7}{200}$$

6. Which point on the number line shows the tax rate in County S?

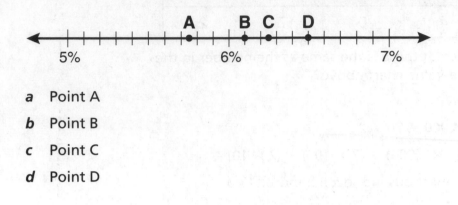

   a   Point A

   b   Point B

   c   Point C

   d   Point D

7. What fraction is equivalent to the sales tax rate in County P?

   a $\frac{1}{20}$

   b $\frac{1}{15}$

   c $\frac{1}{10}$

   d $\frac{1}{5}$

To convert a percent to a fraction, write the percent as a fraction with a denominator of 100. Then reduce. For example:

$$25\% = \frac{25}{100} = \frac{1}{4}$$

8.

1,000s	100s	10s	1s
4	0	7	2

Which of these is the same as the number in the place-value chart above?

a   472

b   4,000 + 70 + 2

c   (4 × 1,000) + (7 × 100) + (2 × 10)

d   four thousand seven hundred two

9.   Which of these is the same as the expression shown in the box below?

$$(2 \times 10^4) + (3 \times 10^2) + (7 \times 10) + (4 \times 1)$$

a   2,374

b   20,374

c   23,074

d   200,374

10. Which of these scales shows an amount greater than $\frac{3}{4}$ pound?

0.739	0.812	0.346	0.501
a	*b*	*c*	*d*

11. A cabinet maker needs to drill a hole in a cabinet door for a handle. The diameter of the hole must be $\frac{1}{8}$ inch so the handle will fit tightly. Which of these is less than $\frac{1}{8}$ inch?

    a $\frac{1}{16}$ inch

    b $\frac{1}{4}$ inch

    c $\frac{3}{8}$ inch

    d $\frac{1}{2}$ inch

Apply

To compare fractions that have different denominators, rewrite the fractions with a common denominator, then compare the numerators. For example: Which fraction is greater, $\frac{3}{7}$ or $\frac{1}{2}$?

$$\frac{3}{7} \times \frac{2}{2} = \frac{6}{14} \qquad \frac{1}{2} \times \frac{7}{7} = \frac{7}{14}$$

The numerator 7 is greater than the numerator 6; therefore, $\frac{1}{2}$ is greater than $\frac{3}{7}$.

Three sizes of dish soap are shown below. Study the pictures.
Then do Numbers 12 through 15.

1.25 liters   2 liters   5 liters

12. The dish soap company plans to add an extra-large size that
    contains 20% more than the large size. How much dish soap
    will the extra-large size contain?

    a   6 liters

    b   7 liters

    c   10 liters

    d   25 liters

13. The amount of dish soap in the small container is what percent
    of the amount in the large container?

    a   12.5%

    b   17.5%

    c   25%

    d   35%

14. Kenny bought the medium-size dish soap. It lasted for 12 weeks.
At this rate, how long would the large size last?

   a 15 weeks

   b 24 weeks

   c 25 weeks

   d 30 weeks

15. Which of these is another way to show the amount of dish soap
in the small container?

   a $1\frac{1}{8}$ liters

   b $1\frac{1}{4}$ liters

   c $1\frac{3}{8}$ liters

   d $1\frac{2}{5}$ liters

Decimals can be written as fractions with denominators that are powers of 10. For example, 0.75 is the same as $\frac{75}{100}$. Notice that the number of digits to the right of the decimal point is the same as the number of zeros in the denominator.

Reminder

16. Ron's apartment has an area of 1,200 square feet. The living room has an area of 400 square feet. What fraction of the area of the apartment is in the area of the living room?

   a $\frac{1}{2}$

   b $\frac{1}{3}$

   c $\frac{1}{4}$

   d $\frac{1}{6}$

17. Cara went on a business trip by airplane. She spent 9 days in California, 3 days in Iowa, 20 days in New York, and 4 days in Arizona. What fraction of the total trip did she spend in Arizona?

   a $\frac{1}{4}$

   b $\frac{1}{8}$

   c $\frac{1}{9}$

   d $\frac{1}{12}$

18. The ratio of adults to children in a pizza parlor is 2 to 5. If there are 10 adults in the pizza parlor, how many children are there?

    a   4

    b 15

    c 20

    d 25

19. Dinah went fishing and caught some trout. The ratio of rainbow trout to brown trout was 5:2. If Dinah caught 6 brown trout, how many rainbow trout did she catch?

    a   9

    b 10

    c 12

    d 15

A proportion consists of two equal ratios. For example, $\frac{1}{2} = \frac{3}{6}$ is a proportion. It can also be written as 1:2 = 3:6.

Reminder

20. The Alvarez family is looking at a scale model of the house they are buying. The model measures 6 inches by 12 inches. The actual house measures 30 feet by 60 feet. What is the scale of the model house?

a   1:30

b   1:45

c   1:60

d   1:72

21. A public radio station has 2,000 regular listeners. Approximately 65% of these listeners gave money to the radio station during a pledge drive. About how many listeners gave money?

a   850

b   1,150

c   1,300

d   1,500

To find a percent of a number, convert the percent to a decimal, then multiply. For example:

90% of 50 = 0.9 × 50 = 45

22. James spent $18 at a restaurant. He wants to calculate 15% of $18 for the tip. Which expression will give 15% of $18?

   a $18 × 0.15

   b $18 × 1.5

   c $18 ÷ 0.15

   d $18 ÷ 1.5

23. The retail price of a watch is $20. The store will add 10% sales tax. How much will the watch cost with tax?

   a $20.20

   b $20.10

   c $22.00

   d $21.00

24. A chiropractor finds that four out of five of his new patients returned for a second visit. Which of these is $\frac{4}{5}$ expressed as a percent?

   a 75%

   b 80%

   c 85%

   d 90%

To convert a fraction to a percentage, rewrite the fraction with a denominator of 100. For example:

Tip

$$\frac{3}{4} = \frac{75}{100} = 75\%$$

For Numbers 25 through 29, write your answers.

25. Write the number thirty-seven and two hundredths as a decimal.

_____

26. Rachel's rent was increased from $600 to $630. By what percent was her rent increased?

_____

27. What fraction is represented by Point A on the number line?

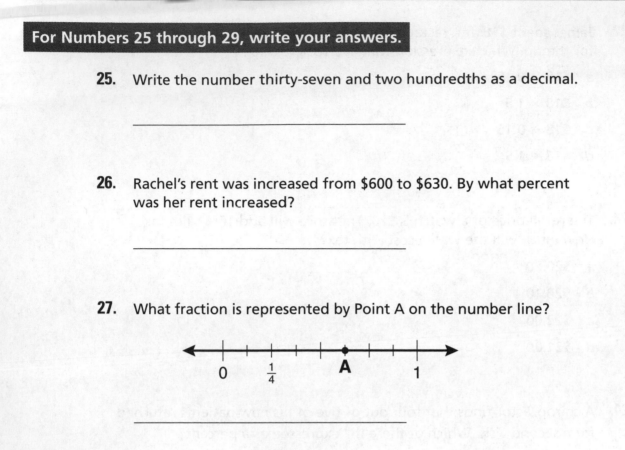

_____

The numbers on a number line increase as you move from left to right.

Reminder

Three candidates have entered an election for a position on the school board. A group of 500 registered voters were asked which candidate they preferred. The table below shows the results of this poll. Study the table. Then do Numbers 28 and 29.

School Board Election Poll

Candidate	Number of Votes
Sandra Alvarez	180
Deborah Chang	170
Ben Steiner	150
Total	**500**

28. What percent of the voters preferred Deborah Chang?

     _____

29. According to this poll, if 10,000 people vote in the election, how many can be expected to vote for Sandra Alvarez?

     _____

COMPUTATION IN CONTEXT

Computation in context is the process of finding the answers to a variety of real-life problems. We do this by using addition, subtraction, multiplication, or division.

Computation in context includes subskills, such as Whole Numbers, Decimals, and Fractions.

Look at this example of computation in context. Choose your answer.

EXAMPLE	ANSWER
Mark bought one package of ground beef weighing 3.26 pounds and one package weighing 1.82 pounds. What was the total weight of the ground beef Mark bought?	• **Answer a** is **not** correct. No regrouping was done.
	• **Answer b** is **not** correct. Two mistakes were made in regrouping.
a 4.08 pounds	• **Answer c** is correct. The two weights can be added as follows:
b 4.18 pounds	
c 5.08 pounds	$$\begin{array}{r} \overset{1}{3.26} \\ + 1.82 \\ \hline 5.08 \end{array}$$
d 5.18 pounds	
	• **Answer d** is **not** correct. An extra tenth was regrouped into the tenths place.

Do these computation in context problems.
First, try Numbers 1 and 2 for practice.

1. Each painter on a painting crew earns $6.45 per hour. If three painters work for three hours each, what is the amount of their combined wages?

   a $19.35

   b $38.70

   c $57.97

   d $58.05

   ANSWER *d* is correct. Each painter earned 3 × $6.45 = $19.35, and since there were 3 painters, multiply $19.35 by 3 to get a total of $58.05.

2. To start his garden, Darren bought $\frac{3}{4}$ ton of soil and $\frac{1}{3}$ ton of manure. What was the total weight of the soil and manure?

   a $\frac{7}{8}$ ton

   b $\frac{11}{12}$ ton

   c $1\frac{1}{12}$ tons

   d $1\frac{1}{8}$ tons

   ANSWER *c* is correct. To add $\frac{3}{4}$ and $\frac{1}{3}$, rewrite each fraction with a denominator of 12, then add: $\frac{3}{4} + \frac{1}{3} = \frac{9}{12} + \frac{4}{12} = \frac{13}{12} = 1\frac{1}{12}$.

Now you are ready to do more problems. The answers to the problems in this section can be found in the back of this workbook.

The table below shows the attendance at two baseball games. Study the table. Then do Numbers 3 and 4.

Baseball Attendance

Day	Attendance
Saturday	28,867
Sunday	35,280

3. What was the total attendance for the two games?

   a 63,047

   b 63,147

   c 64,047

   d 64,147

4. How many more people attended Sunday's game than Saturday's game?

   a 6,413

   b 6,423

   c 7,413

   d 7,423

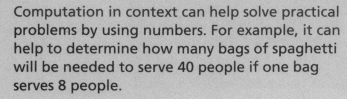 Computation in context can help solve practical problems by using numbers. For example, it can help to determine how many bags of spaghetti will be needed to serve 40 people if one bag serves 8 people.

5. A steel bar 9.45 centimeters long is cut into two parts. If one part of the bar is 2.86 centimeters, how long is the other part?

a 6.59 centimeters

b 6.69 centimeters

c 7.59 centimeters

d 7.69 centimeters

6. A group of 6 hospital employees participated in a walk-a-thon to raise money for the hospital. They each walked the same distance for a total of 20.7 miles. How far did each employee walk?

a 3.4 miles

b 3.45 miles

c 3.5 miles

d 3.55 miles

When adding or subtracting decimals, line up the decimal points. For example:

Reminder

$$\begin{array}{cc} 38.5 \\ \text{correct} - 2.17 \end{array} \qquad \begin{array}{cc} 38.5 \\ \text{incorrect} - 2.17 \end{array}$$

A city has plans to construct a new parking garage. The city surveyed 250 residents to find out what they think about the plan. The table below shows the results of the survey. Study the table. Then do Numbers 7 through 9.

Parking Garage Survey

Opinion	Number of People
In Favor	80
Against	120
Undecided	50
Total	**250**

7. What fraction of the residents surveyed are in favor of the parking garage?

 a $\frac{1}{80}$

 b $\frac{4}{25}$

 c $\frac{8}{25}$

 d $\frac{4}{5}$

8. Revenue from the parking garage is expected to be about
    $15,000 per month. At this rate, what would be the revenue
    for one year?

    a $18,000

    b $180,000

    c $1,800,000

    d $18,000,000

9. The estimated cost of building the parking garage is $9,000,000.
    The cost would be shared equally by 4 organizations. How much
    money would each organization pay?

    a $225,000

    b $250,000

    c $2,250,000

    d $2,500,000

If a total amount is to be divided into equal parts, you can use
division to find the amount of each part.

Reminder

The monthly budget for a nonprofit organization is shown below. Study the budget. Then do Number 10.

Monthly Budget

Rent......................................$750.00	
Utilities................................$170.00	
Supplies..............................$250.00	
Transportation....................$200.00	
Salaries............................$2,400.00	
Other..................................$450.00	
Total	**$4,220.00**

10. The nonprofit organization received a grant of $30,000. For how many months will the grant money cover the monthly budget?

   a   7 months

   b   8 months

   c   14 months

   d   15 months

11. What is the total length of the running trail shown below?

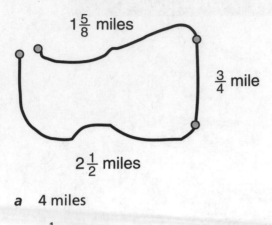

1$\frac{5}{8}$ miles

$\frac{3}{4}$ mile

2$\frac{1}{2}$ miles

a   4 miles

b   4$\frac{1}{8}$ miles

c   4$\frac{5}{8}$ miles

d   4$\frac{7}{8}$ miles

A restaurant offers four types of pasta, as shown on the menu below. Study the menu. Then do Numbers 12 through 14.

PASTA MENU

Spaghetti $7.50
Penne $7.50
Fettuccine $8.45
Ravioli $9.75

For Numbers 12 through 16, write your answers.

12. What would be the total cost for one plate of each type of pasta? (Ignore tax and tip.)

_____

13. What would be the total cost for 3 plates of spaghetti and 3 plates of penne? (Ignore tax and tip.)

_____

14. Michael has a coupon that takes $\frac{1}{3}$ off the price of a plate of ravioli. How much money will he save by using this coupon?

_____

15. A recipe calls for $\frac{3}{4}$ cup of butter. Frances wants to use only $\frac{1}{2}$ this amount. How much butter should she use?

_____

16. Mrs. Chiu paid her nephew $6.00 per hour to mow the lawn. It took him a total of 2.5 hours. How much money did Mrs. Chiu pay her nephew?

_____

ESTIMATION

Estimation is the process of finding an approximate answer rather than an exact answer to a calculation. When an exact answer is not needed, it is often quicker and easier to use an estimate.

Estimation includes subskills, such as Estimation, Rounding, and Reasonableness of Answer.

Look at these examples of estimation. Choose your answer for each problem.

EXAMPLE	ANSWER
Which of these is the best estimate of 392.2 × 0.5? a 150 b 200 c 400 d 2,000	• **Answer a** is **not** correct. The number 392.2 was rounded to 300, then multiplied by 0.5. A better estimate is obtained if 392.2 is rounded to 400. • **Answer b** is correct. The number 392.2 can be rounded to 400, and 400 × 0.5 = 200. • **Answer c** is **not** correct. The number 392.2 was rounded to 400, and 0.5 was rounded to 1: 400 × 1 = 400. • **Answer d** is **not** correct. The number 400 was multiplied by 5 instead of by 0.5.

EXAMPLE	ANSWER

In 1999, there were 1,508 students at a high school. By the year 2000, the number of students had increased by 9.7%. Which of these is the best estimate of the number of students in the year 2000?

a   150

b   1,500

c   1,600

d   1,650

- **Answer *a* is not** correct. This is the approximate increase in the number of students.

- **Answer *b* is not** correct. This is the approximate number of students in 1999.

- **Answer *c* is not** correct. This is an increase of only 100 students during 1999. The increase was actually about 150 students.

- **Answer *d* is correct.** The increase was about 10% of 1,500, or about 150 students. Since there were about 1,500 students in 1999, adding 150 students gives a total of about 1,650 students in the year 2000.

In many situations an exact amount is not needed, but an estimate may be helpful. One might say, "There were about 100 people watching the soccer game," or "Buy a chicken that weighs about 4 pounds," or "Dinner will cost about $8.00 per person." These are all examples of estimates.

Chicken Dinner

$7.99 per person

**Do these estimation problems.
First, try Numbers 1 and 2 for practice.**

1. Jolene has opened a new shoe store. She has mailed 1,525 letters to local residents inviting them to the store's Grand Opening, and expects about 5% of these people to attend. About how many of these people does Jolene expect to attend the Grand Opening?

   a   25

   b   75

   c   250

   d   750

   ANSWER *b* is correct. The number 1,525 can be rounded to 1,500. To find 5% of 1,500, you can convert 5% to a decimal, then multiply: $0.05 \times 1,500 = 75$.

2. A wrench has an opening that measures 0.4375 inch. What is this measurement rounded to the nearest tenth of an inch?

   a   0.4 inch

   b   0.438 inch

   c   0.44 inch

   d   0.5 inch

   ANSWER *a* is correct. The first digit after the decimal point is in the tenths place. Since the digit to the right (3) is less than 5, we round 0.4375 down to get 0.4000 or 0.4.

Now you are ready to do more problems. The answers to the problems in this section can be found in the back of this workbook.

The table below shows the areas of the world's oceans in units of million square miles. Study the table. Then do Numbers 3 and 4.

Areas of the World's Oceans

Ocean	Area (million square miles)
Arctic	4.8
Antarctic	7.6
Indian	28.4
Atlantic	31.5
Pacific	63.8

3. Which of these is the best estimate of the total area of the world's oceans?

    a   between 90 and 120 million square miles

    b   between 120 and 150 million square miles

    c   between 150 and 180 million square miles

    d   between 180 and 210 million square miles

4. Which of these is the best estimate of how many times larger the Atlantic Ocean is than the Arctic Ocean?

    a   4

    b   5

    c   6

    d   8

The table below shows how much electricity a family used each month for a year. Study the table. Then do Numbers 5 through 7.

Electricity Use

Month	Electricity Use in Kilowatt-Hours (kWh)
January	644
February	613
March	467
April	380
May	363
June	465
July	582
August	615
September	533
October	440
November	509
December	598

5. Which of these is the best estimate of the total amount of electricity used for the year?

   a 4,800 kWh

   b 6,000 kWh

   c 7,200 kWh

   d 8,400 kWh

6. The family pays $0.11 per kilowatt-hour for electricity. Which of these is the best estimate of the amount they paid for electricity in July?

   a $30

   b $45

   c $60

   d $75

7. Which of these is the best estimate of the average daily use of electricity in January?

   a   12 kWh

   b   15 kWh

   c   20 kWh

   d   23 kWh

8. Roland bought a coat that was on sale for 40% off. The original price was $79.00. Which of these is the best estimate of the amount of money he saved by buying the coat on sale?

a $2.00

b $3.20

c $20.00

d $32.00

To estimate a percent of an amount, begin by rounding the percent and/or the amount. Then convert the percent to a decimal and multiply.

9. Which of these is the best estimate of 3,910.3 ÷ 4.2?

    a   10

    b   100

    c   1,000

    d 10,000

To round a number to a certain place value, look at the digit to the right of that place value. If the digit is less than 5, leave the rounded place value digit as is, and change all the digits to the right to zeros. For example, 6,349 rounded to the nearest hundred is 6,349 ≈ 6,300.

If the digit to the right of the place value is 5 or greater, add a one to the rounded place value digit, and change all the digits to the right to the zeros. For example, 6,362 rounded to the nearest hundred is 6,362 ≈ 6,400.

10. Lee rounded 7,835 to the nearest 100. Kate rounded the number to the nearest 1,000. What was the difference between their rounded numbers?

a 40

b 100

c 200

d 800

Reminder

To round numbers, you must understand place value.
The chart below shows the order of some place values.

Hundred Thousand	Ten Thousand	Thousand	Hundred	Ten	One	Tenth	Hundredth	Thousandth	Ten Thousandth
__	__	2 ,	4	6	8 .	7	5	__	__

Tom owns a landscaping business. He charges customers
$12 per hour. Do Numbers 11 and 12 about Tom's business.

11. A customer wants Tom to put in a new lawn. Tom expects the job to take
between 70 and 80 hours of work. Which of these is the most reasonable
estimate for the total amount he will charge?

   a $400

   b $750

   c $1,100

   d $1,300

12. One month Tom completed four large jobs, with earnings of $624, $492,
$612, and $384, respectively. Which of these is the best estimate of
Tom's total earnings for the four jobs?

   a $1,900

   b $2,000

   c $2,100

   d $2,200

For Numbers 13 through 15, write your answers.

13. Chris spent $528.85 on supplies for a job she is working on. What is this amount rounded to the nearest ten dollars?

_____

14. What is 213.075 rounded to the nearest hundredth?

_____

15. Six friends spent a total of $35.76 on food for a barbecue. If they share the cost equally, about how much will each pay (to the nearest dollar)?

_____

The table below shows the October rainfall amounts for 8 years in a certain town. Do Number 16, and then write your answer.

October Rainfall

Year	Rainfall Total (in inches)
1992	2.6
1993	4.8
1994	1.5
1995	2.7
1996	1.4
1997	4.5
1998	3.3
1999	2.5

16. To the nearest inch, what is the average October rainfall in this town?

_____

To estimate an average for a set of numbers, begin by finding an estimate of the sum. Then divide the estimated sum by the number of items in the set.

MEASUREMENT

Measurement involves the use of tools such as rulers, scales, thermometers, and clocks to find information. These tools are marked in units that allow us to measure length, width, height, weight, temperature, and time. There are two measurement systems commonly used in the United States—the metric system (meters, grams, etc.) and the customary system (feet, pounds, etc.).

Measurement includes subskills, such as Time, Perimeter, Area, Rate, Convert Measurement Units, and Angle Measure.

Look at these examples of measurement. Choose your answer for each problem.

EXAMPLE	ANSWER
Nicole wants to install wall-to-wall carpet in her bedroom, which measures 12 feet by 15 feet. What is the area of her bedroom? a 27 square feet b 54 square feet c 180 square feet d 360 square feet	• **Answer a** is **not** correct. The numbers were added. • **Answer b** is **not** correct. The numbers were added, then doubled. • **Answer c** is correct. The correct formula, $A = l \times w$, was used to find the area. $12 \times 15 = 180$ • **Answer d** is **not** correct. The number was doubled after multiplying.

EXAMPLE	ANSWER
How many rectangular floor tiles, each measuring 4 inches by 6 inches, will be required to cover a rectangular floor measuring 10 feet by 12 feet? *a* 720 *b* 600 *c* 360 *d* 60	• **Answer *a*** is correct. $4 \times 6 = 24$ sq. in. (area of one tile), and $10(12) \times 12(12) = 17{,}280$ sq. in. (area of the floor); therefore $\frac{17{,}280}{24} = 720$ tiles. • **Answer *b*** is **not** correct. This would be the answer if only 5 tiles were needed to cover 1 square foot. • **Answer *c*** is **not** correct. This would be the answer if only 3 tiles were needed to cover 1 square foot. • **Answer *d*** is **not** correct. The area of one tile, 24 square inches, was converted to 2 square feet, which is incorrect.

Knowing how to measure is one of the most useful math skills you will ever learn. It can help you find out the weight of a package you want to mail, the size of a room you want to paint, or even how many miles you have run around a track.

**Do these measurement problems.
First, try Numbers 1 and 2 for practice.**

1. Alyssa is setting bricks in place for a chimney. It takes her about 30 seconds to set each brick. At this rate, how many bricks can she set in 1 hour?

   a 120 bricks

   b 180 bricks

   c 240 bricks

   d 300 bricks

   ANSWER *a* is correct. There are (60)(60) or 3,600 seconds in 1 hour. Alyssa can set 1 brick in 30 seconds. Divide 3,600 by 30 to determine the number of bricks she can set in 1 hour (120).

2. A group of workers are picking strawberries. After picking from 8:00 A.M. to 10:00 A.M., the group has picked $\frac{1}{3}$ of the strawberries. At this rate, and if the workers take a one-hour lunch break, at what time will they finish picking all the strawberries?

   a 1:00 P.M.

   b 2:00 P.M.

   c 3:00 P.M.

   d 4:00 P.M.

   ANSWER *c* is correct. In 2 hours, the group picked $\frac{1}{3}$ of the strawberries. At this rate, they should pick the remaining $\frac{2}{3}$ of the strawberries in 4 hours. The 4 hours of work plus the one-hour lunch break total 5 hours. They should finish at 3:00 P.M., which is 5 hours after 10:00 A.M.

Now you are ready to do more problems. The answers to the problems in this section can be found in the back of this workbook.

3. When receiving a call, Anna's cell phone rings once every 4 seconds. At this rate, how many times would the cell phone ring in 1 minute?

    a 10

    b 15

    c 20

    d 25

4. Snow began falling at 10:40 P.M. and continued until 5:30 A.M. For how long did it snow?

    a 6 hours and 10 minutes

    b 6 hours and 50 minutes

    c 7 hours and 10 minutes

    d 7 hours and 50 minutes

There are 60 seconds in 1 minute, and 60 minutes in 1 hour.

Reminder

A paving company is repaving the parking lot shown in the diagram. Study the diagram. Then do Numbers 5 through 8.

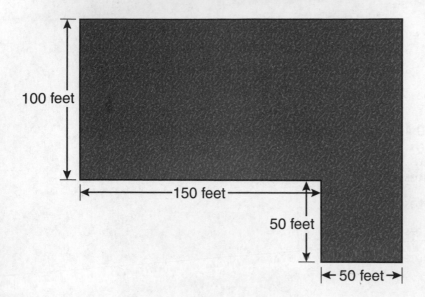

100 feet

150 feet

50 feet

50 feet

5. The paving company put a curb around the outside of the parking lot. What was the length of the curb?

a 350 feet

b 550 feet

c 600 feet

d 700 feet

6. It takes 15 minutes to pave 100 square feet. At this rate, how long does it take to pave 1,000 square feet?

a   2.5 hours

b   2 hours

c   1.5 hours

d   1 hour

7. On Monday, the paving crew started work at 7:45 A.M. They worked $4\frac{1}{2}$ hours, took a half-hour lunch break, and then worked 4 more hours. At what time did they stop working?

a   3:45 P.M.

b   4:15 P.M.

c   4:45 P.M.

d   5:15 P.M.

8. What is the total area to be paved?

a   17,500 square feet

b   20,000 square feet

c   22,500 square feet

d   30,000 square feet

To find the area of a rectangle, multiply the length by the width. The answer will be in square units.

Reminder

9. How much fencing is needed to go around the perimeter of the garden?

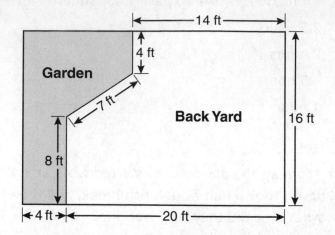

a   23 feet

b   45 feet

c   49 feet

d   69 feet

10. A bucket of water weighs 7,439 grams. How many kilograms of water does the bucket weigh?

a   less than 1 kilogram

b   between 7 and 8 kilograms

c   between 70 and 80 kilograms

d   more than 7,000 kilograms

1 kilogram = 1,000 grams

Reminder

11. What is the length of $\overline{BC}$?

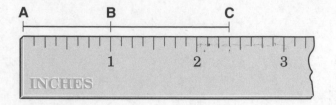

a $1\frac{3}{8}$ inches

b $1\frac{3}{4}$ inches

c $2\frac{3}{8}$ inches

d $2\frac{1}{2}$ inches

12. What is the area of a square rug with a length of 6 feet?

a 12 square feet

b 24 square feet

c 36 square feet

d 42 square feet

13. What is the area of the shaded shape shown below?

a 12 square units

b 13 square units

c 14 square units

d 15 square units

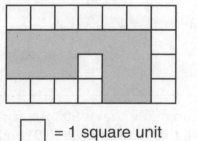

☐ = 1 square unit

Use the clock to do Numbers 14 and 15.

14. Which of these is the measure of the angle formed by the hands shown on the clock?

    a   45°

    b   60°

    c   90°

    d   180°

15. What type of angle is shown by the hands on the clock?

    a   right

    b   acute

    c   obtuse

    d   straight

Reminder

A **right** angle is an angle that is 90°. An **acute** angle is an angle that is greater than 0° and less than 90°. An **obtuse** angle is an angle that is greater than 90° and less than 180°.

16. Which of these open fans forms an obtuse angle?

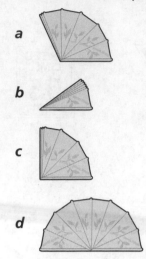

a

b

c

d

Use these traffic signs to do Number 17.

17. Which sign shape contains a right angle?

   a stop sign

   b railroad sign

   c yield sign

   d speed limit sign

The Cruz family is planning to mow their lawn. The diagram below shows the measurements of the lawn. Study the diagram. Then do Numbers 18 and 19, and write your answers.

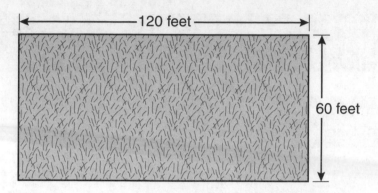

18. What is the length of the lawn, in yards?

_____

19. What is the area of the lawn, in square feet?

_____

There are 12 inches in 1 foot, and 3 feet in 1 yard.

Reminder

GEOMETRY AND SPATIAL SENSE

Geometry and spatial sense involves determining the relationships, properties, and measurements of all sorts of shapes, points, lines, angles, plane figures, and solid figures.

Geometry and Spatial Sense includes subskills, such as Symmetry, Plane Figures, Visualization, Spatial Reasoning, Parallel, Perpendicular, Triangles, and Angles.

Look at these examples of geometry and spatial sense. Choose your answer for each problem.

EXAMPLE	ANSWER

Which of these is a right angle?

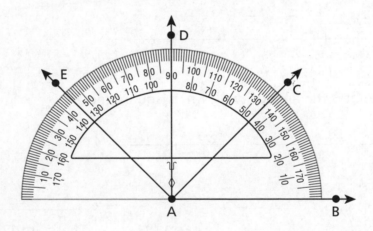

a ∠EAB

b ∠CAB

c ∠DAC

d ∠EAC

- **Answer a is not** correct. A right angle has a measure of 90°. Since the measure of ∠EAB is 135°, it's not a right angle.

- **Answer b is not** correct. The measure of ∠CAB is 45°.

- **Answer c is not** correct. The measure of ∠DAC is also 45°.

- **Answer d** is correct. The measure of ∠EAC is 90°, so it is a right angle.

EXAMPLE	ANSWER

In △PQR, m∠P = 40° and m∠Q = 60°. What is the measure of ∠R?

a   40°

b   60°

c   80°

d   100°

- **Answer a** is **not** correct. The sum of the angle measures of △PQR must be 180° (40° + 60° + 40° = 140°).

- **Answer b** is **not** correct. The sum of the angle measures of △PQR must be 180° (40° + 60° + 60° = 160°).

- **Answer c** is correct. Since the sum of the measures of ∠P and ∠Q equal 100°, the measure of ∠R must be 80° in order for the sum of the angles to equal 180°.

- **Answer d** is **not** correct. The measures of ∠P and ∠Q were added.

Geometry terms are used when saying things such as "The driveway meets the street at a right angle." Geometry can also be used to figure out distances that are hard to measure, such as the length and width of a yard or the height of a building.

**Do these geometry and spatial sense problems.
First, try Numbers 1 and 2 for practice.**

1. Which of these figures could contain only 2 right angles?

   a trapezoid

   b rectangle

   c parallelogram

   d right triangle

   ANSWER *a* is correct. One leg of a trapezoid could be perpendicular to the bases, forming only 2 right angles. A rectangle and a parallelogram could contain 4 right angles. A right triangle can contain only 1 right angle.

Reminder

A trapezoid is a quadrilateral with 1 pair of parallel sides. The parallel sides are called bases of the trapezoid. A parallelogram is a quadrilateral with 2 pairs of parallel sides.

The diagram below shows two triangles formed by diameters $\overline{AB}$ and $\overline{CD}$.

2. If the triangles were formed by any two diameters, which of these statements would **not** necessarily be true?

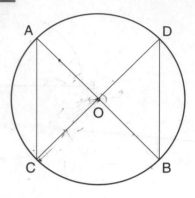

a $\overline{AC} = \overline{BD}$

b $\overline{AB} = \overline{CD}$

c ∠AOC and ∠BOD are right triangles.

d ∠AOC and ∠BOD are isosceles triangles.

ANSWER *c* is correct. The statements in choices *a, b,* and *d* must be true, but there is no reason why ∠AOC and ∠BOD must be right triangles.

Now you are ready to do more problems. The answers to the problems in this section can be found in the back of this workbook.

Look at the circle. Then do Numbers 3 and 4.

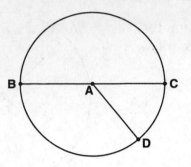

A diameter of a circle is also a chord of the circle.

Tip

3. What is the name of $\overline{BC}$ on the circle?

   a area

   b radius

   c diameter

   d circumference

4. What is the name of $\overline{AC}$ on the circle?

   a chord

   b diameter

   c radius

   d arc

5. Which of these figures is a hexagon?

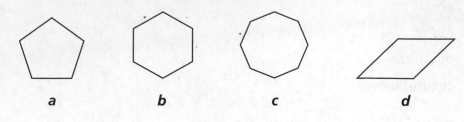

a   b   c   d

6. Which of these triangles below appears to be congruent to the shaded triangle?

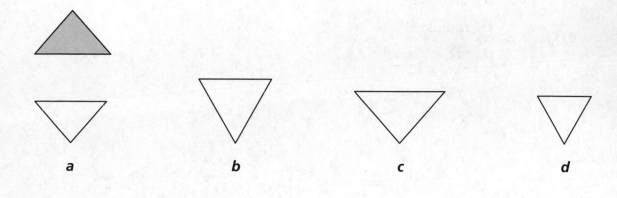

a   b   c   d

Congruent figures have the same shape and size.

Reminder

7. According to the marked measurements, which of these figures is a rhombus?

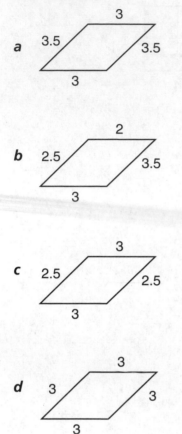

8. Laura made a cardboard figure in the shape of a cylinder for her son's kindergarten class. She cut three shapes out of cardboard and put them together to make the cylinder. What three shapes did she cut out?

    a 2 circles, 1 triangle

    b 2 circles, 1 rectangle

    c 1 circle, 2 triangles

    d 1 circle, 2 rectangles

9. Which two shaded figures are congruent?

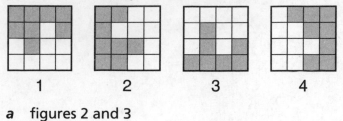

1   2   3   4

  a figures 2 and 3

  b figures 1 and 3

  c figures 2 and 4

  d figures 1 and 2

10. Which of these statements is true
about △MNO?

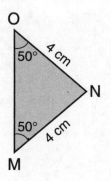

  a $\overline{ON} = \overline{OM}$

  b $\overline{OM}$ = 4 centimeters

  c ∠MNO = 80°

  d △MNO is an equilateral triangle.

In any triangle, the sum of the
angle measures is always 180°.

Reminder

11. If figure ABCD is similar to RSTU, what is the length of $\overline{DC}$?

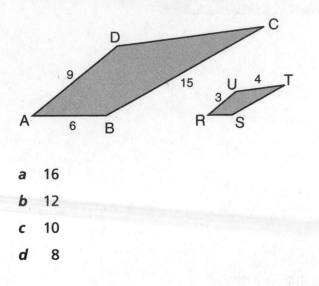

a 16

b 12

c 10

d 8

If two figures are similar, their side lengths are proportional. For example, these triangles are similar:

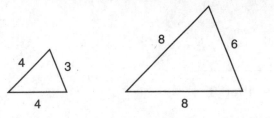

Some proportions are $\frac{4}{3} = \frac{8}{6}$, or $\frac{4}{8} = \frac{3}{6}$, or $\frac{8}{8} = \frac{4}{4}$.

Tip

In the diagram below, $\overline{AB}$ is perpendicular to $\overline{CD}$.
Study the diagram. Then do Numbers 12 through 14.

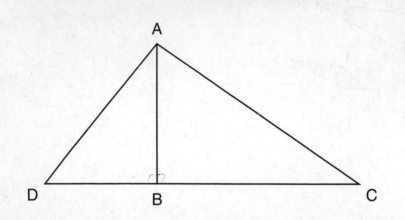

12. Which of these best describes ∠ACB?

   a   acute

   b   obtuse

   c   right

   d   exterior

Reminder

An acute angle is greater than 0°
and less than 90°.

13. Which of these best describes △ABC?

    a   equilateral triangle

    b   congruent triangle

    c   obtuse triangle

    d   right triangle

For Number 14, write your answer.

14. What is the degree measure of ∠ABD?

_____

Perpendicular lines meet
to form right angles.

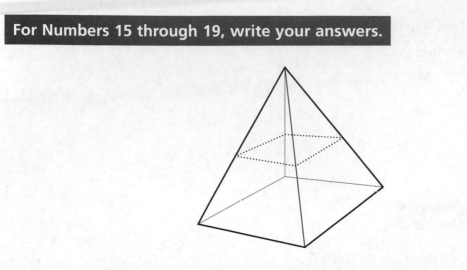

15. If the rectangular pyramid above is sliced along the dotted line, how many edges will the bottom part have?

_____

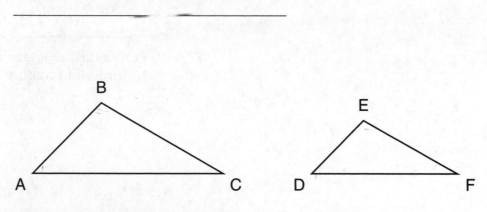

16. In the diagram above, △ABC and △DEF are similar. If ∠BAC measures 40°, what is the measure of ∠EDF?

_____

In the diagram below, O is the center of the circle. Study the diagram. Then do Numbers 17 through 19.

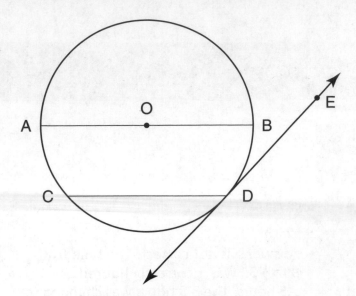

17. What is the name of $\overline{OB}$?

_____

18. If the diameter of this circle is 12 centimeters, what is the radius in centimeters?

_____

19. Which line is a tangent to the circle?

_____

A line segment that passes through the center of a circle and has its endpoints on the circle is called the **diameter** of the circle. Every diameter is twice the radius in length.

Reminder

DATA ANALYSIS

Data is numerical information displayed in graphs, charts, tables, and diagrams. *Data analysis* is the process of gathering meaning from the data.

Data Analysis includes subskills, such as Bar, Line, Circle Graph, Table, Chart, Diagram, and Conclusions from Data.

Look at these examples of data analysis. Choose your answer for each problem.

EXAMPLE	ANSWER

This table shows the rates at a parking garage. Edna drove into the garage at 8:00 A.M. and left at 1:30 P.M. How much did Edna pay for parking?

PARKING RATES

First hour....................................$3.00
Each additional 1/2 hour..........$1.00
Maximum fee per day.............$15.00

a $10.00

b $12.00

c $14.00

d $15.00

- **Answer a is not correct.** The time from 9 to 1:30 was incorrectly figured as 3.5 hours. The 3.5 hours was changed to 7 half hours and charged $7: $3 + $7 = $10.

- **Answer b is correct.** The charge for the first hour is $3. The time from 9 to 1:30 (4.5 hours) was changed to 9 half hours and charged $9: $3 + $9 = $12.

- **Answer c is not correct.** The time from 8 to 1:30 (5.5 hours) was changed to 11 half hours and charged $11: $3 + $11 = $14.

- **Answer d is not correct.** The time from 8 to 1:30 was incorrectly figured as 6.5 hours. The 6.5 hours was changed to 13 half hours and charged $13: $3 + $13 = $16. The answer given was $15 because that is the maximum charge per day.

Jessica has her own business taking care of the plants in office buildings. The flier below shows the rates Jessica charges. Study the flier.

JESSICA'S
PLANT CARE
Plant Care for Office Buildings

Rates: $30 per week, plus
$2 per week per plant

Results Guaranteed!

EXAMPLE

ANSWER

The owner of one building gave Jessica a check for $400. What additional information is needed to find out how many plants Jessica takes care of in that building?

a the number of offices in the building

b the number of weeks of plant care the check covered

c the number of customers Jessica has

d the number of plants that can be bought for $400

- **Answer *a* is not** correct. The number of offices has no effect on the number of plants being cared for.

- **Answer *b* is correct.** If the number of weeks of plant care is known, this number can be multiplied by $30. The product can then be subtracted from $400. Finally, the difference can be divided by $2 to find the number of plants that Jessica takes care of.

- **Answer *c* is not** correct. The number of customers has no effect on the number of plants being cared for.

- **Answer *d* is not** correct. The number of plants that can be bought has no relevance to the problem.

Do these data analysis problems.
First, try Numbers 1 and 2 for practice.

The graph below shows the water absorption of an
insulating material when it is submerged in water for 20 days.
Study the graph. Then do Numbers 1 and 2.

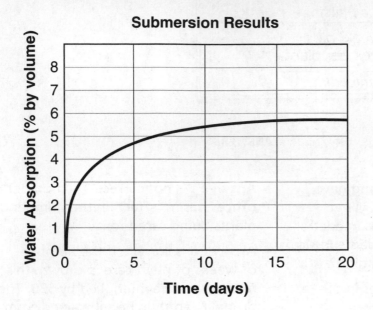

1. During which time period does the graph show
the greatest rate of increase in water absorption?

a   0–5 days

b   5–10 days

c   10–15 days

d   5–20 days

ANSWER *a* is correct. The portion of the graph that rises
most steeply is the portion between 0 days and 5 days.

2. About how many days did it take for the water absorption
to reach 5%?

a 4.5 days

b 5 days

c 6.5 days

d 7 days

ANSWER *c* is correct. The curved line graph intersects
the 5 percent line between six and seven days.

**Now you are ready to do more problems. The answers to the
problems in this section can be found in the back of this workbook.**

You might say that data analysis tells "the real story behind the numbers."
If a newspaper story shows a graph which displays how the price of gas
has risen over the past year, data analysis helps you figure out exactly
how much the prices have changed.

Trina drove to the city to visit her family. The graph below shows the time and distance she traveled. Study the graph. Then do Numbers 3 through 5.

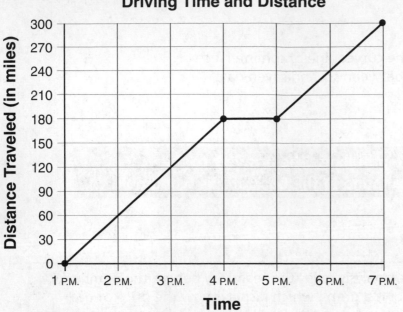

Driving Time and Distance

3. How far had Trina driven by 7:00 P.M.?

a   120 miles

b   180 miles

c   300 miles

d   350 miles

4. Which of these could explain what occurred from 4:00 P.M. to 5:00 P.M.?

   a Trina drove more slowly.

   b Trina drove faster.

   c Trina stopped to rest.

   d Trina was driving across a flat desert.

5. What was Trina's average rate of speed from 1:00 P.M. to 4:00 P.M.?

   a 45 miles per hour

   b 50 miles per hour

   c 55 miles per hour

   d 60 miles per hour

To find the average rate of speed, divide the distance traveled by the time traveled.

The graph below shows the average high and low temperatures for a certain city in January, April, July, and October.
Use this graph to do Numbers 6 and 7.

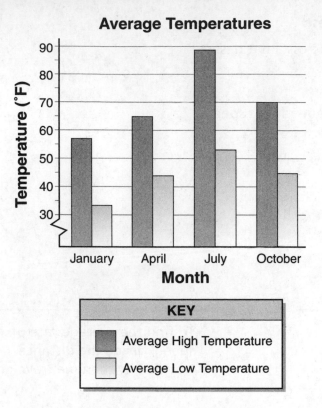

Average Temperatures

6. During which month is the difference between the average high and low temperatures the greatest?

   a January

   b April

   c July

   d October

7. Which of these is the best estimate of the mean (average) low temperature for the four months shown in the graph?

   a 35°F

   b 45°F

   c 60°F

   d 70°F

8. Look at the table below showing recent population data for a small city.

Brooksville Population

Year	Population	Percent Increase
1980	78,567	13%
1984	91,147	16%
1988	97,517	7%
1992	111,139	14%
1996	122,286	10%
2000	136,980	12%

During which four-year period did the greatest increase in population occur?

a 1980–1984

b 1984–1988

c 1988–1992

d 1996–2000

The table below shows the number of customers during lunch hour at four different restaurants. Study the table. Then do Numbers 9 through 11.

Food Court Customers

Restaurant	Number of Customers
Mama's Pizza	35
Big Al's BBQ	51
Taqueria Rosa	45
Stir-Fry Supreme	73

For Numbers 9 and 10, write your answers.

9. What is the total number of customers at the four restaurants?

_____

10. At Taqueria Rosa, 60% of the customers order a burrito. What is the probability that a customer will **not** order a burrito?

_____

11. Which of these circle graphs best represents the information in the table?

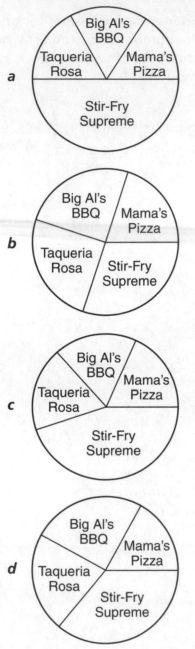

a

b

c

d

In a circle graph, each section represents a fraction or percentage of the total.

Reminder

For Number 12, write your answer.

12. A computer store kept track of its computer and printer sales for one week. The Venn diagram below shows the number of customers who bought a computer, a printer, or both a computer and a printer. How many customers in all bought a computer?

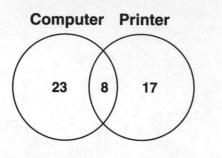

Computer Printer

23   8   17

_____

The overlapping portion of a Venn diagram represents items that belong to both sets.

Reminder

NOTES

STATISTICS AND PROBABILITY

Statistics involves the collection, organization, and interpretation of numerical data.

Probability is the likelihood of a certain event occurring, and is expressed as a ratio or a fraction.

Statistics and Probability includes subskills, such as Mean, Mode, Median, Range, and Independent Events.

Look at these examples of statistics and probability. Choose your answer for each problem.

EXAMPLE	ANSWER

The line plot shows the prices of five brands of breakfast cereal

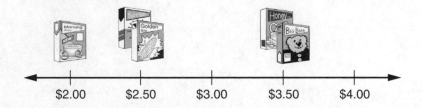

$2.00 $2.50 $3.00 $3.50 $4.00

What is the median of the data?

a $1.50

b $2.50

c $2.80

d $3.00

- **Answer *a* is not** correct. This is the range of the data.

- **Answer *b*** is correct. The five brand prices listed in order are $2.00, $2.50, $2.50, $3.50, $3.50. The median is the middle price.

- **Answer *c* is not** correct. This is the mean (or average) of the data.

- **Answer *d* is not** correct. This is the middle value marked on the number line.

EXAMPLE	ANSWER

A number cube with its sides numbered 1 through 6 is rolled twice. What is the probability of rolling a 2 and then a 5?

a $\frac{1}{36}$

b $\frac{1}{30}$

c $\frac{1}{25}$

d $\frac{11}{30}$

- **Answer a** is correct. The probability of a 2 being rolled is $\frac{1}{6}$, and the probability of a 5 being rolled is $\frac{1}{6}$. $\frac{1}{6} \times \frac{1}{6} = \frac{1}{36}$

- **Answer b** is **not** correct. An error was made in one of the probabilities. $\frac{1}{6} \times \frac{1}{5} = \frac{1}{30}$

- **Answer c** is **not** correct. An error was made in both probabilities. $\frac{1}{5} \times \frac{1}{5} = \frac{1}{25}$

- **Answer d** is **not** correct. An error was made in one of the probabilities, and the probabilities were added instead of multiplied. $\frac{1}{6} + \frac{1}{5} = \frac{11}{30}$

Do these statistics and probability problems.
First, try Numbers 1 and 2 for practice.

1. Joe says the average (mean) of his age and Martha's age is 20. If Martha is 18, how old is Joe?

   a 19

   b 22

   c 38

   d 40

ANSWER *b* is correct. $\frac{18 + x}{2} = 20$; $x = 22$

2. Ricardo has 7 white T-shirts and 3 gray T-shirts in a drawer. If he pulls out one T-shirt without looking, what is the probability that it will be gray?

   a $\frac{1}{3}$

   b $\frac{1}{4}$

   c $\frac{3}{7}$

   d $\frac{3}{10}$

ANSWER *d* is correct. There are a total of 10 T-shirts in the drawer. Since 3 of them are gray, the probability Ricardo will pull out a gray T-shirt is $\frac{3}{10}$.

Now you are ready to do more problems. The answers to the problems in this section can be found in the back of this workbook.

3. Sherrie had 7 quarters, 5 dimes, 11 pennies, and 7 nickels mixed in a coin purse. Without looking, she took one coin out of the purse. What is the probability that the coin she took out was a dime or a penny?

a $\frac{1}{30}$

b $\frac{1}{6}$

c $\frac{11}{30}$

d $\frac{8}{15}$

When writing a probability as a fraction, use the total of all the possible outcomes (total of all the items) as the denominator of the fraction. For the numerator, use the total number of outcomes (or items) for which you are finding the probability. Then reduce the fraction, if possible.

Reminder

4. Drew has a mixed bag of apples containing the following:

- 3 Pippin apples
- 4 Red Delicious apples
- 3 Pink Lady apples
- 2 Granny Smith apples

Drew reached into the bag without looking and removed 1 apple. What is the probability that the apple he removed was a Red Delicious apple?

a $\frac{1}{4}$

b $\frac{1}{3}$

c $\frac{1}{2}$

d $\frac{2}{3}$

5. The table below shows the scores given to Jill by judges in a gymnastics competition.

Jill's Gymnastics Scores

Judge	1	2	3	4	5	6	7	8	9	10
Score	9.2	8.9	8.8	9.0	9.2	9.3	9.0	9.2	9.5	8.9

What is the mode for Jill's gymnastics scores?

a 8.9

b 9.0

c 9.1

d 9.2

The mode for a set of numbers is the number that appears most often.

Tip

6. The table below shows three types of carpet sold to 100 customers.

Carpet Purchased

Carpet Type	Number of People
Berber	20
High shag	50
Low shag	30

Each customer who bought carpet received a coupon for a grand prize drawing. What is the probability that the winning coupon was from a customer who purchased Berber carpet?

a $\frac{1}{20}$

b $\frac{1}{5}$

c $\frac{2}{5}$

d $\frac{1}{3}$

7. The table below shows the length of several movies at a multi-screen theater.

The Orbitz Theater

Screen	Length (in hours)
A	1.25
B	1.75
C	1.25
D	2
E	2
F	1.25
G	2.75
H	1.75

What is the median length of the movies showing at the Orbitz Theater?

a 1.25 hours

b 1.50 hours

c 1.75 hours

d 2.00 hours

The median for a set of numbers is the middle number, after all numbers have been placed in ascending order.

Reminder

8. Charlie works for the city recreation department. He is writing a questionnaire to use in a survey to find out what recreational sports are most popular in his community. Which of these questions would give Charlie the most accurate results?

   a What do you do in your free time?

   b What sport do you play the most often?

   c What sport do you watch the most on television?

   d What sport team did you sign up for last summer?

9. The table below shows the golf scores made by Charlene after 10 rounds of golf.

Charlene's Golf Scores

Round	1	2	3	4	5	6	7	8	9	10
Score	89	96	102	92	88	96	100	82	96	89

What is the mode for Charlene's golf scores?

   a 89

   b 93

   c 94

   d 96

10. Sandra compared home equity loan interest rates at several banks. The table below shows the interest rates at the banks.

Bank Interest Rates

Bank	Interest Rate
Creekside Bank	5.2%
Hillside Bank	5.9%
Bank of the Plains	6.2%
Bank of the Mesa	6.6%
Seaside Bank	6.8%
Bank of the Desert	7.5%
Lakeside Bank	5.9%
Bank of the Valley	7.9%

What is the range for the interest rates?

a 2.7%

b 5.9%

c 6.4%

d 6.5%

Reminder

The range for a set of numbers is the difference between the highest (greatest) number and the lowest (least) number.

11. Jessica takes care of plants in a building that has seven offices. The list below shows how many plants are in each office. What is the median number of plants in the building?

2, 13, 5, 4, 12, 2, 11

a   2

b   5

c   7

d   11

12. The table below shows the magazines and the number of subscriptions Mike's company sold over a period of 6 months.

Magazine Subscriptions

Magazine	Number Sold
Sports Highlights	300
Boating Pleasure	100
Climbing Adventures	240
Golf Techniques	360

Each person who bought a subscription was given an opportunity to win a prize in a drawing. What is the probability that the person who won the drawing was a person who bought a subscription to *Sports Highlights* or to *Climbing Adventures*?

a $\frac{6}{25}$

b $\frac{3}{10}$

c $\frac{23}{50}$

d $\frac{27}{50}$

13. A box has a mixture of 3 yellow cards, 1 blue card, and 2 green cards. What is the probability of someone, without looking, drawing a green card, keeping it, and then drawing a yellow card?

 a $\frac{1}{9}$

 b $\frac{1}{5}$

 c $\frac{1}{3}$

 d $\frac{14}{15}$

14. The table below shows the amount of rainfall in Smithfield County over an eight-week period.

Smithfield County Rainfall (in inches)

Week 1	Week 2	Week 3	Week 4	Week 5	Week 6	Week 7	Week 8
3.2	3.0	3.2	3.4	2.5	2.5	3.2	3.0

What is the median of the rainfall for the eight-week period?

 a 0.9

 b 3.0

 c 3.1

 d 3.2

For Numbers 15 through 19, write your answers.

15. Laura and Charlie are taking four days to drive 1,300 miles from San Diego, California, to Austin, Texas. On average, how many miles will they cover per day?

   _____

16. Of the 12 people on a bus, 3 are going to the mall. If a person on the bus is chosen at random, what is the probability that the person is **not** going to the mall?

   _____

17. Alphabet tiles that spell out the word "MATHEMATICS" are mixed in a bag. If someone, without looking, removes a tile from the bag, what is the probability that the tile will **not** be an M or an A?

   _____

18. The map below shows the distances between the towns Belinda visited.

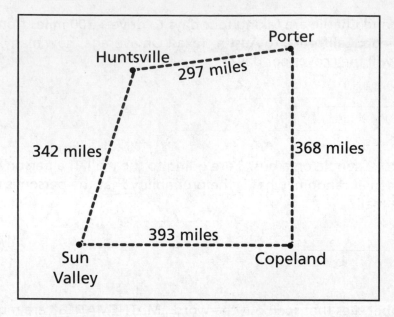

It took Belinda 14 days to travel from Sun Valley, to Copeland, to Porter, to Huntsville, and back to Sun Valley. What is the mean (average) number of miles Belinda traveled per day?

_____

To find the mean (average) of a set of numbers, find the sum of the set and divide it by the number of items in the set. For example, the mean of 8, 9, and 4 is:

$$\frac{8 + 9 + 4}{2} = \frac{21}{3} = 7$$

19. The chart below shows the admission prices to Fun Land Amusement Park.

Fun Land Amusement Park

General Admission (ages 7–59)	$40
Seniors (ages 60+)	$30
Children (ages 3–6)	$25
Children under 3	Free

Pedro Martinez and his family are going to Fun Land Amusement Park for Pedro's twelfth birthday. The ages for the Martinez family members are listed below.

- Mr. Martinez   44
- Ms. Martinez   42
- Mr. Martinez, Sr.   74
- Pedro   12
- Yolanda   6

What is the mean (average) price the family paid for admission to the park?

_____

PATTERNS, FUNCTIONS, ALGEBRA

A *pattern* is the arrangement of numbers or elements in a particular order or sequence. The order or sequence depends on a specific rule, such as "add 3" or "multiply by 5."

A *function* is a set of ordered pairs (a relation) in which the value of the first number (the domain) is paired with exactly one value of the second number (the range).

Algebra is the process of using letters (variables or boxes) to represent unknown numbers. The value of the variables can be found by performing mathematical operations using the rules of algebra.

Patterns, Functions, Algebra includes subskills, such as Variable, Expression, Equation, Function, and Linear Equations.

Look at these examples of patterns, functions, and algebra. Choose your answer for each problem.

EXAMPLE	ANSWER

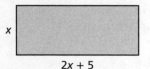

$2x + 5$

Which of these expressions gives the area of the rectangle above?

a $3x + 5$

b $6x + 10$

c $2x^2 + 5$

d $2x^2 + 5x$

- **Answer a** is **not** correct. The length and width were added instead of multiplied.

- **Answer b** is **not** correct. This is the perimeter of the rectangle instead of the area.

- **Answer c** is **not** correct. Both terms of $2x + 5$ must be multiplied by x.

- **Answer d** is correct. To find the area, the length and width must be multiplied: $x(2x + 5) = 2x^2 + 5x$.

EXAMPLE	ANSWER

What number should go in the boxes to make this number sentence true?

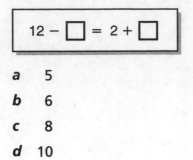

a   5

b   6

c   8

d   10

- **Answer a** is correct: $12 - 5 = 2 + 5$.
- **Answer b** is **not** correct: $12 - 6 \neq 2 + 6$.
- **Answer c** is **not** correct: $12 - 8 \neq 2 + 8$.
- **Answer d** is **not** correct: $12 - 10 \neq 2 + 10$.

The table below shows the steady increase in the number of cells in a test tube over a period of time. Study the table. Then do Number 1.

Cells in Test Tube

Time	Number of Cells
2:00 P.M.	3
3:00 P.M.	6
4:00 P.M.	12
5:00 P.M.	24

1. If the pattern of the growth of cells continues, how many cells will be in the test tube at 8:00 P.M.?

   a 48

   b 60

   c 96

   d 192

   ANSWER d is correct. The number of cells in the test tube is doubling each hour. At 6:00 P.M. there will be 48 cells, at 7:00 P.M. there will be 96 cells, and at 8:00 P.M. there will be 192 cells.

2. If $y = 6x - 2$, what is the value of y when $x = 3$?

   a   5

   b   6

   c 16

   d 20

ANSWER *c* is correct. The 3 is substituted for the variable *x*, and then the equation is solved for the variable *y* :

$$y = 6(3) - 2$$
$$y = 18 - 2$$
$$y = 16$$

Now you are ready to do more problems. The answers to the problems in this section can be found in the back of this workbook.

Algebra skills may be used when checking an electric bill, a telephone bill, or determining how many hot dogs and buns can be bought for $20.

3. What number is missing from the number pattern below?

> 80, 72, 64, _____, 48, 40, 32, . . .

a 54

b 56

c 60

d 62

4. Which symbol goes in the box to complete this number sentence?

5 ☐ 8 = 13

a <

b +

c −

d ×

Reminder

Some number patterns are formed by adding, subtracting, multiplying, or dividing by a certain number. For example, the pattern 2, 5, 8, 11, 14, . . . is formed by repeatedly adding 3. The pattern 100, 50, 25, 12.5, . . . is formed by repeatedly dividing by 2.

5. A carpenter cut off $\frac{2}{5}$ of a board. Which of these number sentences shows how to find the fraction of the board that was left after the board was cut?

a ☐ $= 1 - \frac{2}{5}$

b ☐ $= 1 \times \frac{2}{5}$

c ☐ $= 1 + \frac{2}{5}$

d ☐ $= 1 \div \frac{2}{5}$

6. What symbol goes in the box to make the number sentence true?

$$77 \ \boxed{} \ 11 < 8$$

a −

b +

c ×

d ÷

The symbol "<" means "less than." The symbol "≥" means "greater than or equal to."

Reminder

A plumber charges $40 for each visit, plus $25 per hour for the work he does. The table below shows the total charges based on the amount of hours the plumber works. Study the table. Then do Numbers 7 through 9.

Plumbing Charges

Hours Worked	Total Charges
1	$65
2	$90
3	$115
4	$140

7. What will the total charges be if the plumber works for 5 hours?

   a $125

   b $165

   c $205

   d $325

8. The plumber charged $240 for one visit. How many hours did the plumber work?

a 6

b 7

c 8

d 9

9. Which equation shows the relationship of *T* to *h*?

T = the total dollar-amount charged
h = the number of hours worked

a $T = 65h$

b $T = 65 + h$

c $T = 40 + 25h$

d $T = 25 + 40h$

The product of two variables (or a number and a variable) may be written without the multiplication sign. For example:

$$a \times b = ab$$
$$5 \times z = 5z$$

Reminder

10. A jacket costs $24, plus 8% sales tax. Which of these number sentences could be used to find the total cost, in dollars, of the jacket?

a ☐ = $24 + 0.08 × $24

b ☐ = $24 + 0.8 × $24

c ☐ = $24 − 0.08 × $24

d ☐ = $24 − 0.8 × $24

11. What symbol goes in the box to make the number sentence true?

0.51 + 0.50 ☐ 1.0

a >

b <

c =

d ≤

12. The lease payment on the Winstons' car is $250 per month. In addition, they spend an average of $40 per week on gasoline and maintenance for the car.

Which equation gives their total yearly expenses (T) for the lease, gasoline, and maintenance?

  a $T = \$290 \times 12$

  b $T = \$290 \times 52$

  c $T = \$250 \times 12 + \$40 \times 52$

  d $T = \$250 \times 52 + \$40 \times 12$

13. A market sold 120 cases of canned peaches and canned apricots. The number of cases of canned apricots was 50 more than the number of cases of canned peaches.

If x represents the number of cases of peaches sold by the market, which of these expressions gives the number of cases of canned apricots sold by the market?

  a $x \div 50$

  b $x + 50$

  c $x - 50$

  d $50x$

For Numbers 14 through 16, write your answers.

Input	➡ Output
3	0
6	6
7	8
11	16
13	20
17	28

14. The table above shows Input numbers that have been changed by a certain rule to get Output numbers. What is the rule for changing the Input numbers to Output numbers?

_____

When finding the rule used to make an Input-Output table, make sure the rule works for every row of the table.

Reminder

15. Jenna's long-distance calling plan charges $10.00 each month for the first 200 minutes and $0.08 per minute thereafter. Last month, Jenna made 300 minutes of long-distance calls. How much was her long-distance telephone bill?

_____

16. What value of y makes the equation below true?

$$2y - 8 = 10$$

_____

To solve an equation such as $4x + 10 = 22$, start by subtracting 10 from both sides. Then divide both sides by 4:

$$4x + 10 = 22$$
$$4x = 12$$
$$x = 3$$

Tip

PROBLEM SOLVING AND REASONING

Problem solving and reasoning utilizes the processes to formulate problems, to determine and apply strategies to solve problems, and to evaluate and justify solutions.

Problem Solving and Reasoning includes subskills, such as Solve Problem, Identify Missing/Extra Information, and Evaluate Solution.

Look at these examples of problem solving and reasoning. Choose your answer for each problem.

EXAMPLE	ANSWER
Clare's water company charges a monthly fee of $16.33, plus $0.94 for each of the first 50 gallons used. After 50 gallons, the company charges $1.08 for each gallon used. How much will Clare's water bill be if she uses 72 gallons of water in one month? a $77.76 b $84.01 c $87.09 d $94.09	• **Answer a** is **not** correct. (72 × $1.08 = $77.76) • **Answer b** is **not** correct. (72 × $0.94 = $67.68); ($16.33 + $67.68 = $84.01) • **Answer c** is correct. [$16.33 + (50 × $0.94) + (22 × $1.08)]; ($16.33 + $47 + $23.76 = $87.09) • **Answer d** is **not** correct. (72 × $1.08 = $77.76); ($16.33 + $77.76 = $94.09)

EXAMPLE	ANSWER

Beth is going to build a fence around her rectangular garden. The length of her garden is 15 yards. Fencing costs $1.25 per yard. If Beth paid $62.50 for the fencing, which of these equations can be used to find the width of her garden?

a $62.50 = 2(w + 15)($1.25)

b $62.50 = 2 + (w + 15)($1.25)

c $62.50 = (w + 15)($1.25)

d $62.50 = (2w + 15)($1.25)

- **Answer a is correct.** The perimeter of the garden, represented by $2(w + 15)$, should be multiplied by the cost per yard ($1.25). This product should equal the total cost ($62.50).

- **Answer b is not correct.** The sum of the length and width should be multiplied by 2, not added to 2.

- **Answer c is not correct.** The sum of the length and width should be multiplied by 2. This equation represents only half of the garden.

- **Answer d is not correct.** The length (15 yards) should also be multiplied by 2.

To solve problems, read the entire problem carefully. Plan a strategy to solve the problem, and then use the strategy. State the answer to the problem, and then check the answer to make sure it is reasonable.

Reminder

Do these problem solving and reasoning problems. First, try Numbers 1 and 2 for practice.

1. A pet store has 20 angelfish and guppies for sale in a fish tank. The store charges $2.49 per fish and $7.50 for a fishbowl. Josh bought 5 guppies, some angelfish, and 2 fishbowls. What information is needed to find the total cost for the fish and fishbowls?

   a the number of guppies in the fish tank

   b the number of angelfish bought

   c the size of the fishbowls

   d the type of fish bought

   ANSWER *b* is correct. The number of angelfish bought is needed to find the total cost.

To find what additional information is needed to solve a problem, first try to solve the problem with only the given information.

2. During a basketball game, $\frac{3}{4}$ of the seats in the basketball arena were occupied, and 200 seats were unoccupied. Which of these equations can be used to find the total number of seats (s) in the basketball arena?

   a $\frac{3}{4}s = 200$

   b $\frac{3}{4}(200) = s$

   c $\frac{1}{4}(200) = s$

   d $\frac{1}{4}s = 200$

ANSWER *d* is correct. Since $\frac{3}{4}$ of the seats were occupied, $\frac{1}{4}$ of the seats (200) were unoccupied.

Now you are ready to do more problems. The answers to the problems in this section can be found in the back of this workbook.

3. Autolube received a shipment of 12 cases of motor oil. Each case contains 12 quarts of motor oil. For each oil change, 5 quarts of motor oil are needed. How many oil changes can be completed using the oil from this shipment?

a   5

b   24

c   28

d   29

4. Autolube charges $24 for each oil change. They usually do from 15 to 20 oil changes each morning, and from 20 to 25 oil changes each afternoon. Which of these could be the total amount of money Autolube earns for oil changes on any one day?

a $360

b $480

c $600

d $960

5. David is going to plant grass in his front yard. The front yard is a rectangular shape with a length of 15 feet and width of 10 feet. It will take 4 packets of lawn seed to cover one square foot of ground. If each packet of lawn seed costs $0.53, how much will lawn seed for the entire front yard cost?

a $19.88

b $31.80

c $106.00

d $318.00

Study the menu for Food Time Deli. Use the chart to do Numbers 6 and 7.

Food Time Deli Menu

Sandwiches	Drinks
Tuna............ $2.60	Juice.... $1.00
Turkey......... $2.95	Soda.... $1.50
Club............. $3.95	
Roast Beef... $4.50	

6. Anna bought 2 of the same kind of sandwich and 1 drink at the Food Time Deli. She spent a total of $6.90. What kind of sandwich did Anna buy?

   a tuna sandwich

   b turkey sandwich

   c club sandwich

   d roast beef sandwich

7. One Tuesday, the Food Time Deli sold 23 club sandwiches, which was 12% of all the sandwiches sold that day. It cost the Food Time Deli $1.35 to make one club sandwich.

   Which of these is **not** needed to find the amount of profit the deli made on club sandwiches that Tuesday?

   a the percent of all the sandwiches sold that were club sandwiches

   b the number of club sandwiches that were sold

   c the cost to make a club sandwich

   d the price to buy a club sandwich

The chart below shows the admission prices to the History Museum. Study the chart. Then do Number 8.

History Museum Admission

Adult	$15
Youth (11–18 years)	$12
Child (5–10 years)	$8
Under 5	free

8. Ms. Jackson took her sixth-grade class to the History Museum. On the field trip, there was 1 adult for every 4 students. What additional information is needed to find the total entrance cost for Ms. Jackson's class?

   a the ages of the students

   b the price of a child's ticket

   c the day and time of their visit

   d the number of students in Ms. Jackson's class

Chancy's Carpets placed the ad shown below about a special spring offer. Study the ad. Then do Number 9.

Chancy's Carpets

$14 per
sq yd

Replace your carpet this spring and save!

20% off, March only
$200 savings (on 200 square yards or more), April only
OR
1 bedroom free, May only

9. Which of these is **not** needed to find the cost of a carpet that Rob purchased during this special spring offer?

   a the price of carpet per square yard

   b the month he plans to carpet the house

   c the number of bedrooms that are in his house

   d the number of square yards of carpet he needs

10. Tom's Tree Service cut a fallen tree trunk into logs for firewood. The logs were then loaded into the back of a truck. The length of the tree trunk was 20 feet. Which of these must be known to determine the number of logs that were cut?

 a the weight of each log

 b the length of each log

 c the volume of the back of the truck

 d the number of logs it takes to fill the back of the truck

11. In checking her daughter's math homework, Mary found an error in the problem shown below.

$$6 \times (2 + 5) - 18 \div 2$$

Step 1	$6 \times 7 - 18 \div 2$
Step 2	$42 - 18 \div 2$
Step 3	$24 \div 2$
Step 4	12

In which step did Mary's daughter make an error?

 a Step 1

 b Step 2

 c Step 3

 d Step 4

Reminder

The following order of operations must be followed when simplifying expressions.

1) Simplify expressions contained within grouping symbols, such as parentheses and brackets. When simplifying these expressions, be sure to follow rules 2, 3, and 4 in their given order.
2) Evaluate all exponents.
3) Do all multiplication and division from left to right. Perform the operation as soon as it appears.
4) Do all addition and subtraction from left to right. Perform the operation as soon as it appears.

Phillip works at a department store and completed the order form shown below. Study the order form. Then do Number 12.

Order Form

Item	Quantity	Price Each	Cost
Cups	10	$1.25	$12.50
Saucers	8	$1.50	$12.00
Bowls	9	$1.75	$15.50
Plates	12	$2.00	$24.00
		Subtotal	$64.00
		Tax 6%	$3.84
		Total	$67.84

12. In checking his work, Phillip noticed he made an error. What error did Phillip make in the order form?

   a He did not find the correct subtotal.

   b He did not find the correct tax amount.

   c He did not find the correct cost for the bowls.

   d He did not find the correct cost for the plates.

13. The perimeter of a rectangle is 84 centimeters. The length of the rectangle is 20 centimeters. Which of these equations can be used to find the width (*w*) of the rectangle?

   a $2(20) + w = 84$

   b $2(20 + w) = 84$

   c $20 + 2w = 84$

   d $2(20w) = 84$

For Numbers 14 through 18, write your answers.

14. Angela goes to the library every 4 days. Darren goes to the library every 6 days, and Joline goes to the library every 8 days. Today, all three are at the library. In how many days will Angela, Darren, and Joline again all be at the library at the same time?

    _____

15. In a survey, 16% of the people said country music was their favorite. If 152 people said country music was their favorite, how many people were surveyed?

    _____

16. Mike makes phone calls to sell magazine subscriptions. For every 8 calls, he sells 3 subscriptions. It takes Mike 30 minutes to make 10 calls. How long will it take Mike to sell 30 subscriptions?

    _____

17. A city bus driver begins her first route at 8:00 A.M. It takes her 1.5 hours to complete the route and return to the station. During the work day, the driver has two 15-minute breaks and a 30-minute lunch break. How many routes does she complete by 4:30 P.M.?

_____

The table below shows Jorge's time card for one week. Study the table. Then do Number 18.

	Monday	Tuesday	Wednesday	Thursday	Friday
Regular hours		8	8	8	8
Overtime hours		2	2		
Holiday hours	8				

18. Jorge earns $8.50 for each regular hour he works at his job. He is paid $1\frac{1}{2}$ times his regular pay for working overtime. He is paid 2 times his regular pay for working on holidays.

How much did Jorge earn for the week shown on the time card?

_____

Question	Answer	MATH COMPUTATION: Multiplication of Whole Numbers, Level D
3	*b*	The product of 747 and 3 is 2,241.
4	*a*	The product of 186 and 9 is 1,674.
5	*c*	The product of 68 and 29 is 1,972.
6	*d*	The product of 563 and 28 is 15,764.
7	*d*	The product of 94 and 24 is 2,256.
8	*d*	The product of 120 and 260 is 31,200.
9		**15,813** The product of 5,271 and 3 is 15,813.
10		**10,500** The product of 350 and 30 is 10,500.
11		**8,460** The product of 470 and 18 is 8,460.
12		**89,232** The product of 507 and 176 is 89,232.

		MATH COMPUTATION: Division of Whole Numbers, Level D
3	*d*	The quotient of 814 divided by 22 is 37.
4	*a*	The quotient of 153 divided by 9 is 17.
5	*c*	The quotient of 72 divided by 6 is 12.
6	*d*	The quotient of 126 divided by 7 is 18.
7	*e*	The quotient of 257 divided by 6 is 42 R5. Since the answer is not given, **e** is correct.
8	*c*	The quotient of 224 divided by 14 is 16.
9	*e*	The quotient of 921 divided by 6 is 153 R3. Since the answer is not given, **e** is correct.
10		**46** The quotient of 368 divided by 8 is 46.
11		**38** The quotient of 608 divided by 16 is 38.
12		**42 R7** The quotient of 385 divided by 9 is 42 R7.

		MATH COMPUTATION: Fractions, Level D
3	*b*	The difference is $\frac{5}{9}$.
4	*c*	The difference is $\frac{3}{7}$.
5	*a*	The product is $\frac{2}{8}$ or $\frac{1}{4}$.
6	*c*	The product is $\frac{6}{36}$ or $\frac{1}{6}$.
7	*d*	The quotient is $\frac{14}{21}$ or $\frac{2}{3}$.
8	*a*	The quotient is $\frac{10}{11}$.

Answer Key

Question	Answer	MATH COMPUTATION: Fractions, Level D (cont.)
9		$8\frac{7}{10}$ The sum is $7\frac{9}{10} + \frac{8}{10} = 7\frac{17}{10} = 8\frac{7}{10}$.
10		$\frac{7}{16}$ The difference is $\frac{13}{16} - \frac{6}{16} = \frac{7}{16}$.
11		$\frac{1}{3}$ The product is $\frac{2}{3} \times \frac{1}{2} = \frac{2}{6}$ or $\frac{1}{3}$.
12		$\frac{4}{5}$ The quotient is $\frac{2}{5} \div \frac{1}{2} = \frac{2}{5} \times \frac{2}{1} = \frac{4}{5}$.

		MATH COMPUTATION: Decimals, Level D
3	c	The sum is 79.39.
4	b	The difference is 18.572.
5	a	The product is 756.86.
6	b	The product is 4,420.78.
7	a	The quotient is 570.
8	a	The quotient is 0.23.
9		**$13.65** The sum of $3.87 and $9.78 is $13.65.
10		**1.091** The difference between 11.112 and 10.021 is 1.091.
11		**0.7098** The product of 0.507 and 1.4 is 0.7098.
12		**160** The quotient of 38.4 divided by 0.24 is equivalent to 3,840 divided by 24, the result of which is 160.

		MATH COMPUTATION: Integers, Level D
3	b	$^-13 - 12 = {}^-13 + {}^-12 = {}^-25$
4	c	$3 - (^-8) = 3 + 8 = 11$
5	b	The product of unlike signs is negative. $^-100 \times 4 = {}^-400$
6	a	The product of like signs is positive. $^-6 \times (^-9) = 54$
7	d	The quotient of like signs is positive. $^-55 \div {}^-5 = 11$
8	b	The quotient of unlike signs is negative. $36 \div {}^-9 = {}^-4$
9		$^-9$ $\;9 + (^-10) + (^-8) = 9 + {}^-18 = {}^-9$
10		**20** $16 - (^-4) = 16 + 4 = 20$
11		$^-42$ $\;{}^-7 \times 2 \times 3 = {}^-7 \times 6 = {}^-42$
12		$^-23$ The quotient of unlike signs is negative. $^-69 \div 3 = {}^-23$

Question	Answer	MATH COMPUTATION: Percents, Level D
3	c	30% of 90 = $\frac{30}{100}$ × 90 = $\frac{2700}{100}$ = 27, or 0.3 × 90 = 27
4	c	40 ÷ 100 = $\frac{40}{100}$ = 40%
5	a	20 ÷ 400 = $\frac{20}{100}$ = $\frac{5}{100}$ = 5%
6	c	7 ÷ 10 = $\frac{7}{10}$ = $\frac{70}{100}$ = 70%
7	e	50 ÷ 0.1 = 500, or 50 ÷ $\frac{10}{100}$ = 50 × $\frac{100}{10}$ = 500 Since the answer is not given, **e** is correct.
8	b	2 ÷ 0.5 = 4, or 2 ÷ $\frac{50}{100}$ = 2 × $\frac{100}{50}$ = 4
9	c	9 ÷ 0.15 = 60, or 9 ÷ $\frac{15}{100}$ = 9 × $\frac{100}{15}$ = 60
10		**60** 12 ÷ 0.2 = 60, or 12 ÷ $\frac{20}{100}$ = 12 × $\frac{100}{20}$ = 60
11		**25%** 8 ÷ 32 = 0.25 = 25%, or $\frac{8}{32}$ = $\frac{1}{4}$ = $\frac{25}{100}$ = 25%
12		**3** 5% × 60 = 0.05 × 60 = 3, or $\frac{5}{100}$ × 60 = $\frac{300}{100}$ = 3

		APPLIED MATHEMATICS: Number and Number Operations, Level D
3	c	802,064,305 is eight hundred two million, sixty-four thousand, three hundred five.
4	b	20,000,000 + 2,000,000 + 100,000 + 5,000 + 700 written in standard form is 22,105,700.
5	d	The rate in County R is 6.75%, and the rate in County T is 7%. The only answer given that is greater than 6.75% and less than 7.0% is 6.9%: 6.75%: < 6.9% < 7.0%
6	c	The tax rate in County S is 6.25%. There are ten equal intervals from 6% to 7%, so each mark represents an increase of 0.1%. Point C is halfway between 6.2% and 6.3%, so it must represent 6.25%.
7	a	The sales tax rate in County P is 5%, which is equal to $\frac{5}{100}$ or $\frac{1}{20}$.
8	b	4 thousands, 0 hundreds, 7 tens, and 2 ones are equal to 4,000 + 70 + 2.
9	b	$2 \times 10^4 + 3 \times 10^2 + 7 \times 10 + 4 \times 1 = 2 \times 10{,}000 + 3 \times 100 + 70 + 4 =$ 20,000 + 300 + 74 = 20,374.
10	b	The fraction $\frac{3}{4}$ is equal to 0.75. The only decimal on any scale that reads more than 0.75 is 0.812.
11	a	Since $\frac{1}{8}$ is equal to $\frac{2}{16}$, $\frac{1}{16}$ must be less than $\frac{1}{8}$.
12	a	One large size is 100%. The extra-large is 20% more, or 120%. Therefore, 120% of 5 liters = 1.2 × 5 = 6 liters.
13	c	1.25 liters is what percent of 5 liters. $\frac{1.25}{5}$ = 0.25 or 25%
14	d	$\frac{2 \text{ liters}}{12 \text{ weeks}} = \frac{5 \text{ liters}}{x \text{ weeks}}$; 2x = 60; x = 30
15	b	1.25 = $1\frac{25}{100}$ = $1\frac{1}{4}$

Answer Key

|---|---|---|
16	b	The living room is 400 sq. ft. out of 1,200 sq. ft. of the apartment, or $\frac{400}{1,200}$, which reduces to $\frac{1}{3}$.
17	c	Cara spent 4 days in Arizona out of a total of 36 days. The fraction $\frac{4}{36}$ reduces to $\frac{1}{9}$.
18	d	$\frac{2 \text{ adults}}{5 \text{ children}} = \frac{10 \text{ adults}}{x \text{ children}}$; $2x = 50$; $x = 25$ children
19	d	$\frac{5 \text{ rainbow}}{2 \text{ brown}} = \frac{x \text{ rainbow}}{6 \text{ brown}}$; $2x = 30$; $x = 15$ rainbow trout
20	c	Since the 6 inches corresponds to the 30 feet, set up a ratio, convert so all units of measure are the same, and then reduce the ratio: $\frac{6 \text{ inches}}{30 \text{ feet}} = \frac{6 \text{ inches}}{30(12) \text{ inches}} = \frac{6 \text{ inches}}{360 \text{ inches}} = \frac{1 \text{ inch}}{60 \text{ inches}} =$ 1:60; or $\frac{6 \text{ inches}}{30 \text{ feet}} = \frac{1}{2}$ foot $\div$ 30 feet $= \frac{1}{2} \times \frac{1}{30} = \frac{1}{60} =$ 1:60
21	c	$0.65 \times 2,000 = 1,300$
22	a	The decimal 0.15 is equal to 15%. The word "of" indicates to multiply, so 18×0.15 will give the tip.
23	c	Multiply $20 \times 0.10 = 2$ to find the tax. Add the tax amount to get the total cost. $20 + 2 = 22$; or Since the price of the watch is 100% and the tax is 10% more, then take 110% of the price of the watch. 110% of $20 = 1.1 \times 20 = 22$
24	b	$\frac{4}{5} = \frac{80}{100} = 80\%$; or $4 \div 5 = 0.8 = 80\%$
25		**37.02** This number is the same as $37 + \frac{2}{100}$, or thirty seven and two hundredths.
26		**5%** To find a percent of increase, divide the increase by the original amount. $\frac{(630 - 600)}{600} = \frac{30}{600} = \frac{5}{100} = 5\%$
27		$\frac{5}{8}$ There are eight equal intervals from 0 to 1, so each interval represents an increase of $\frac{1}{8}$. Point A is located on the fifth interval, so it must represent the fraction $\frac{5}{8}$.
28		**34%** $\frac{170}{500} = \frac{34}{100} = 34\%$
29		**3600** $\frac{180 \text{ Sandra}}{500 \text{ total}} = \frac{x \text{ Sandra}}{10,000 \text{ total}}$; $500x = 1,800,000$; $x = 3,600$ votes for Sandra
		APPLIED MATHEMATICS: Computation in Context, Level D
3	d	$28,867 + 35,280 = 64,147$
4	a	$35,280 - 28,867 = 6,413$
5	a	$9.45 - 2.86 = 6.59$
6	b	$20.7 \div 6 = 3.45$
7	c	There were 80 people out of 250 in favor of the garage: $\frac{80}{250} = \frac{8}{25}$
8	b	There are 12 months in one year, so $15,000 \times 12 = 180,000$.
9	c	$9,000,000 \div 4 = 2,250,000$
10	a	It will cover 7 full months. $30,000 \div 4,220 \approx 7.1$

Question	Answer	APPLIED MATHEMATICS: Computation in Context, Level D (cont.)
11	*d*	$1\frac{5}{8} + \frac{3}{4} + 2\frac{1}{2} = 1\frac{5}{8} + \frac{6}{8} + 2\frac{4}{8} = 3\frac{15}{8} = 4\frac{7}{8}$
12		**$33.20** $7.50 + $7.50 + $8.45 + $9.75 = $33.20
13		**$45** Spaghetti is $7.50 × 3 = $22.50. Penne is $7.50 × 3 = $22.50. The total cost is $22.50 + $22.50 = $45; or Since both pastas are the same price, then multiply 6 by the price of one plate. 6 × $7.70 = $45
14		**$3.25** $9.75 × $\frac{1}{3}$ = $\frac{$9.75}{3}$ = $3.25
15		$\frac{3}{8}$ **cup** The word "of" indicates "to multiply". $\frac{1}{2} × \frac{3}{4} = \frac{3}{8}$
16		**$15.00** $6 × 2.5 = $15
		APPLIED MATHEMATICS: Estimation, Level D
3	*b*	The number for each ocean can be rounded to the nearest ten, and then added. So, 0 + 10 + 30 + 30 + 60 = 130 million square miles. This total falls between 120 million and 150 million square miles.
4	*c*	The area of the Arctic Ocean can be rounded to 5 million square miles, and the area of the Atlantic Ocean can be rounded to 30 million square miles. 30 ÷ 5 = 6
5	*b*	Round off each month's use to the nearest hundred and add to get 6,200 kWh. This sum is nearest to 6,000 kWh.
6	*c*	The amount of electricity used in July can be rounded to 600 kWh. The price paid per kilowatt-hour can be rounded to $0.10; 600 × $0.10 = $60.
7	*c*	The electricity used in January can be rounded to 600 kWh, and the number of days in January can be rounded to 30 kWh. 600 ÷ 30 = 20 kWh
8	*d*	Round the original price of the coat to $80. 40% × $80 = 0.4 × $80 = $32.00
9	*c*	Round 3,910.3 to 4,000 and 4.2 to 4. 4,000 ÷ 4 = 1,000
10	*c*	Kate's rounded number is 8,000. Lee's rounded number is 7,800. The difference is 8,000 − 7,800 = 200.
11	*b*	Round $12 to $10. It may take about 75 hours of work. 75 × $10 = $750
12	*c*	Round each amount to the nearest hundred, and then add. $600 + $500 + $600 + $400 = $2,100
13		**$530** The number 2 is in the tens place, and to its right is the digit 8. Since 8 is greater than 5, the 2 rounds up to 3, and the rest of the digits to the right of 3 become zeros.
14		**213.08** The 7 is in the hundredths place, and the digit to its right is a 5. Therefore, the 7 digit rounds up to 8. The final rounded result is 213.08.
15		**$6** Round the amount spent on food to $36. $36 ÷ 6 = $6
16		**3 inches** Round each rainfall total to the nearest inch and then add to get a total of 25 inches. The average is 25 ÷ 8 = 3.125, which rounded to the nearest inch is 3.

Answer Key

APPLIED MATHEMATICS: Measurement, Level D

Question	Answer	
3	*b*	One minute is 60 seconds: 60 ÷ 4 = 15.
4	*b*	If snow had fallen for 10 more minutes (until 5:40 A.M.) it would have equaled 7 hours. Since it was 10 minutes short of 7 hours, subtract 10 minutes from 7 hours to get 6 hours and 50 minutes.
5	*d*	2(100 + 50) + 2(150 + 50) = 2(150) + 2(200) = 300 + 400 = 700 feet.
6	*a*	To pave an area that is 10 times as large would take 10 times as long. So, 15 minutes × 10 = 150 minutes. 150 ÷ 60 = 2.5 hours.
7	*c*	Add the time worked and the lunch break: 4.5 + 0.5 + 4.0 = 9 hours. Nine hours added to 7:45 A.M. is 4:45 P.M.
8	*c*	Add the area of two rectangles. Rectangle 1: 100 ft × 150 ft = 15,000 sq. ft.; Rectangle 2: 50 ft × 150 ft. = 7,500 sq. ft. Total: 15,000 + 7,500 = 22,500 square feet.
9	*c*	The perimeter is the sum of all the distances around the garden. 10 + 16 + 4 + 8 + 7 + 4 = 49 feet
10	*b*	There are 1,000 grams in a kilogram; so, 7,439 ÷ 1,000 = 7.439 kilograms, which is between 7 and 8 kilograms.
11	*a*	The distance from 1 to 2 is one inch. There are eight equal intervals between each inch, so each interval mark represents an increase of $\frac{1}{8}$ inch. Point C lays three interval marks from the 2-inch mark, so that distance is $\frac{3}{8}$ inch. Add the two distances $(1 + \frac{3}{8})$ to get $1\frac{3}{8}$ inch.
12	*c*	A square has the same length and width, so 6 × 6 = 36.
13	*b*	The area of the entire shape is (7 × 4), or 28 square units. There are 15 unshaded square units. The area of the shaded shape is (28 − 15), or 13 square units.
14	*b*	The angle measure between each two numbers on the clock is (360° ÷ 12), or 30°. The angle measure between 12 and 2 is (30 + 30), or 60°.
15	*b*	The angle shown is less than 90°. An acute angle is greater than 0° and less than 90°.
16	*a*	The angle of the open fan is greater than 90° and less than 180°, and therefore forms an obtuse angle.
17	*d*	The speed limit sign is in the shape of a rectangle. Rectangles have four right angles.
18		**40 yards** There are 3 feet in 1 yard. 120 ÷ 3 = 40 yards.
19		**7,200 sq. ft.** $A = l \times w$; $A = 120 \times 60 = 7,200$

Answer Key

Question	Answer	APPLIED MATHEMATICS: Geometry and Spatial Sense, Level D
3	c	A diameter is a segment which passes through the center of a circle and has endpoints on the circle.
4	c	A radius is a segment which has one endpoint on the center of a circle and one endpoint on the circle.
5	b	A hexagon is a polygon with six sides.
6	a	Congruent triangles have exactly the same shape and size.
7	d	All of the sides of a rhombus must be the same length.
8	b	Two equal circles form the ends of a cylinder, and a rectangle can be wrapped around the two circles to form the middle section.
9	d	If Figure 2 is rotated 90° clockwise, it will show that shaded Figures 1 and 2 have the same size and shape.
10	c	The sum of the angles in a triangle equals 180°. $50° + 50° + n = 180°$; $100° + n = 180°$; $n = 80°$
11	b	Corresponding sides of similar figures are proportional. $\frac{3}{9} = \frac{4}{x}$; $3x = 36$; $x = 12$
12	a	∠ACB is less than 90°, so it is an acute angle.
13	d	Since $\overline{AB}$ is perpendicular to $\overline{CD}$, triangle ABC has an angle that measures exactly 90°, so it is a right triangle.
14		**90°** $\overline{AB}$ is perpendicular to $\overline{CD}$. Perpendicular lines meet to form 90° angles (or right angles).
15		**12** There are 4 edges at the bottom of the solid, 4 at the top, and 4 around the sides, making a total of 12 edges.
16		**40°** ∠EDF corresponds to ∠BAC. The measures of corresponding angles in similar triangles are equal.
17		**Radius** A segment with one endpoint on the center of a circle and the other endpoint on the circle is a radius of that circle.
18		**6 cm** The radius is always one-half the length of the diameter of a circle.
19		**$\overline{DE}$** A tangent is a line that intersects a circle at only one point.

Answer Key

APPLIED MATHEMATICS: Data Analysis, Level D

Question	Answer	
3	c	The point on the graph at 7:00 P.M. corresponds to 300 miles.
4	c	No distance was covered from 4:00 P.M. to 5:00 P.M., so she was not driving.
5	d	rate = $\frac{distance}{time}$; $r = \frac{180}{3} = 60$ miles per hour
6	c	The distance is greatest between the average high and average low for the month of July.
7	b	Round each low temperature to the nearest mark on the scale and then find the average. $35 + 45 + 55 + 45 = 180$; $180 \div 4 = 45$
8	d	From 1996 to 2000, there was an increased of over 14,000. This was the greatest increase of any of the four year periods.
9		**204** $35 + 51 + 45 + 73 = 204$
10		**40% or 0.4 or $\frac{2}{5}$** $100\% - 60\% = 40\% = \frac{40}{100} = \frac{2}{5}$
11	d	The largest section should be Stir-Fry Supreme and the smallest section should be Mama's Pizza. Of the two remaining sections, Taqueria Rosa should be smaller than Big Al's BBQ.
12		**31** $23 + 8 = 31$

APPLIED MATHEMATICS: Statistics and Probability, Level D

Question	Answer	
3	d	There are $(7 + 5 + 11 + 7)$ or 30 coins in all. Of the 30 coins, $(5 + 11)$ or 16 coins are dimes or pennies. Therefore, the probability of selecting a dime or penny is 16 out of 30, or $\frac{16}{30}$ or $\frac{8}{15}$.
4	b	There are $(3 + 4 + 3 + 2)$, or 12 apples in all, of which 4 are red delicious apples. The probability of removing a red delicious apple is 4 out of 12, or $\frac{4}{12}$ or $\frac{1}{3}$.
5	d	The mode is the score that appears most often. The score 9.2 appears 3 times, which is more than any other score.
6	b	There are $(20 + 50 + 30)$, or 100 customers in all who bought carpet, of which 20 customers purchased Berber carpet. The probability that a customer who purchased a Berber carpet had the winning coupon is 20 out of 100, or $\frac{20}{100}$ or $\frac{1}{5}$.
7	c	The median of a set of data is the middle number after the numbers have been placed in ascending order. If there is an even number of data, the median is the average of the two numbers near the middle. In this case, 1.75 and 1.75 are the two numbers near the middle. $\frac{1.75 + 1.75}{2} = 1.75$ hours
8	b	Choice *a* would not give accurate results since some persons may not participate in any sports in their free time. Choice *c* would not give accurate results since some persons may not participate in the sports they watch most often on television. Choice *d* would not give accurate results since some persons may no longer be interested in the sports in which they participated last summer.
9	d	The mode is the score that appears most often. The score 96 appears 3 times, which is more than any other score.

Question	Answer	APPLIED MATHEMATICS: Statistics and Probability, Level D (cont.)
10	*a*	The range for a set of data is the difference between the lowest and highest numbers. In this case, 5.2% is the lowest number, and 7.9% is the highest number. 7.9% − 5.2% = 2.7%
11	*b*	The median of a set of data is the middle number after the numbers have been placed in ascending order. In this case, there are seven numbers, so the fourth number is the middle number. The fourth number in ascending order is 5.
12	*d*	There are (300 + 100 + 240 + 360), or 1,000 magazines sold in all, of which (300 + 240), or 540 are Sport Highlights or Climbing Adventures magazines. The probability of a person who purchased either magazine and also winning the drawing is 540 out of 1,000, or $\frac{540}{1,000}$ or $\frac{27}{50}$.
13	*b*	There are (3 + 1 + 2), or 6 cards in all, of which 2 are green cards. The probability of drawing a green card on the first try is 2 out of 6, or $\frac{2}{6}$ or $\frac{1}{3}$. Since the drawn green card is kept, there are now 5 cards in all, or which 3 are yellow cards. The probability of drawing a yellow card in the next try is 3 out of 5, or $\frac{3}{5}$. The probability of these two drawings occurring in succession is the product of the two probabilities. $\frac{1}{3} \times \frac{3}{5} = \frac{1}{5}$
14	*c*	The median of a set of data is the middle number after the numbers have been placed in ascending order. If there is an even number of data, the median is the average of the two numbers near the middle. In this case, 3.0 and 3.2 are near the middle. $\frac{3.0 + 3.2}{2} = 3.1$
15		**325 miles** $\frac{1,300}{4} = 325$
16		$\frac{9}{12}$ or $\frac{3}{4}$ or **0.75 or 75%** If 3 persons are going to the mall, then (12 − 3), or 9 persons are not going to the mall. The probability of the chosen person not going to the mall is 9 out of 12, or $\frac{9}{12}$ or $\frac{3}{4}$.
17		$\frac{7}{11}$ There are 11 letters in the word "MATHEMATICS", of which 7 letters are not a M or an A. The probability is 7 out of 11, or $\frac{7}{11}$.
18		**100 miles** The total distance traveled is (297 + 342 + 368 + 393), or 1,400 miles. Since the total trip took 14 days, the average miles per day is $\frac{1,400}{14} = 100$ miles.
19		**$35** The total admission paid is ($40 + $40 + $30 + $40 + $25), or $175. Since there are 5 persons in the family, the average price paid for admission is $\frac{$175}{5} = $35.
		APPLIED MATHEMATICS: Patterns, Functions, Algebra, Level D
3	*b*	The pattern is to subtract 8 from each preceding number. 64 − 8 = 56
4	*b*	The sum of 5 and 8 is 13.
5	*a*	To find the amount remaining, the amount cut off $(\frac{2}{5})$ should be subtracted from the whole board (1).
6	*d*	77 ÷ 11 = 7, which is less than 8. The other operations result in a number that is greater than 8.
7	*b*	$40 + 5($25) = $40 + $125 = $165

Question	Answer	APPLIED MATHEMATICS: Patterns, Functions, Algebra, Level D (cont.)
8	c	Subtract the charge for the visit, then divide by the hourly charge. $240 − $40 = $200; $200 ÷ $25 = 8 hours
9	c	The total charged (T) is equal to the cost of the visit ($40) added to the product of $25 and the number of hours (h) worked.
10	a	The total cost is $24 plus the tax amount. The tax amount can be expressed as 0.08 × $24.
11	a	0.51 + 0.50 = 1.01. The sum of the decimals, 1.01, is greater than 1.0.
12	c	The lease payments are monthly, so the yearly expense is $250 × 12. The gasoline and maintenance expenses are weekly, so the yearly expense is $40 × 52. The total yearly expense is the sum of the two expenses.
13	b	There were 50 more cases of apricots sold than peaches. The word "more" immediately following a number indicates "to add".
14		**Subtract 3, then multiply by 2; or multiply by 2, then subtract 6.**
15		**$18.00** The first 200 minutes is $10. The additional 100 minutes are $0.08 each. 100 × $0.08 = $8; $10 + $8 = $18
16		$y = 9$ $2y − 8 + 8 = 10 + 8$; $2y = 18$; $\frac{2y}{2} = \frac{18}{2}$, $y = 9$

		APPLIED MATHEMATICS: Problem Solving and Reasoning, Level D
3	c	The total number of quarts available is (12 × 12), or 144 quarts. For each oil change, 5 quarts are needed. $\frac{144}{5}$ = 28.8, or 28 oil changes
4	d	The least number of oil changes in the morning is 15, and the least in the afternoon is 20. Then (15 + 20), or 35 oil changes are the least that can be completed in one day. The total amount charged for these oil changes would be (35 × $24), or $840. The most number of oil changes in the morning is 20, and the most number in the afternoon is 25. Then (20 + 25), or 45 oil changes are the most that can be completed in one day. The total amount of money charged would be (45 × $24), or $1,080. Therefore, the amount charged for oil changes on any one day should be between $840 and $1,080.
5	d	The area of the lawn is (15 × 10), or 150 square feet. Since 4 packets of lawn seed cover one square foot, then (4 × 150), or 600 packets of lawn seed are needed. One packet of seed cost $0.53. 600 × $0.53 = $318
6	b	It is not possible that Anna bought either club or roast beef sandwiches, as the cost for two of either sandwiches is greater than what she spent. The cost of two tuna sandwiches is (2 × $2.60), or $5.20. The cost of neither drink added to the cost of two tuna sandwiches will add to the total of $6.90. Therefore, she must have bought two turkey sandwiches and one juice drink. 2 × $2.95 = $5.90; $1 + $5.90 = $6.90
7	a	The percent of club sandwiches sold is not needed to find the profit made on club sandwiches.

Question	Answer	APPLIED MATHEMATICS: Problem Solving and Reasoning, Level D (cont.)
8	*d*	The number of students in the class is needed in order to find the total entrance cost.
9	*c*	To find the cost of the carpet during the special offer, you must know the price of the carpet per square yard, and the number of square yards needed. The cost is also affected by the month in which the carpet is purchased. The number of bedrooms in the house has no affect on the cost of the carpet.
10	*b*	The weight of each log, the volume of the truck, and the number of logs that fill the truck have nothing to do with determining the number of logs that were cut from the tree. The length of each log will determine the number of logs cut.
11	*c*	The error was made in step 3 because the order of operations was not followed. The daughter subtracted 18 from 42 instead of first dividing 18 by 2. By dividing first, the daughter would have then subtracted 9 from 42 to obtain the correct answer of 33.
12	*c*	The correct cost for the bowls is ($9 \times \$1.75$), or $15.75. All the other calculations based on the error are correct.
13	*b*	The formula for the perimeter of a rectangle is $P = 2l + 2w$, or $P = 2(l + w)$. By substituting the given values in the second formula, you obtain $84 = 2(20 + w)$.
14		**24 days** To find the number of days, you need to find the lowest common multiple for the numbers 4, 6, and 8. The lowest common multiple is the smallest number into which each of the three numbers will divide. The smallest number is 24.
15		**950 people** All the people surveyed can be represented by the variable (*a*). $16\% \times a = 152$; $a = \frac{152}{0.16}$; $a = 950$
16		**4 hours** $\frac{8 \text{ calls}}{3 \text{ subscriptions}} = \frac{x \text{ calls}}{30 \text{ subscriptions}}$; $x = 80$; $\frac{30 \text{ min}}{10 \text{ calls}} = \frac{x \text{ min}}{80 \text{ calls}}$; $x = 240$ minutes; $\frac{240 \text{ min}}{60 \text{ min}} = 4$ hours
17		**5 routes** The bus driver's work day from 8 A.M. to 4:30 P.M. is 8.5 hours long. The length of time not driving a route is (15 minutes + 15 minutes + 30 minutes), or 60 minutes, or 1 hour. The time left to drive the routes is (8.5 – 1), or 7.5 hours. Each route takes 1.5 hours. $\frac{7.5}{1.5} = 5$ routes
18		**$459** The total number of Jorge's regular hours is (4×8), or 32 hours. He is paid $8.50 per hour, so his total regular pay is ($32 \times \$8.50$), or $272. The total number of overtime hours is (2 + 2), or 4 hours. He is paid 1.5 times his regular pay for overtime, so his total overtime pay is ($4 \times 1.5 \times \$8.50$), or $51. On holidays, he is paid 2 times his regular pay, so his holiday total pay is ($8 \times 2 \times \$8.50$), or $136. $272 + $51 + $136 = $459

Building Skills with TABE®

Tests of Adult Basic Education

Student Answer Booklet

Level D: Math Computation and Applied Mathematics

Name: _____   Date: _____

Organization/Program: _____

PERSONAL STUDY PLAN

Directions: After you have talked with your teacher, circle the skill sections below that you need to work on. Turn to those skill sections in the workbook that match the skill sections circled below. Then find the same skill sections in this answer booklet. Fill in the correct bubble or write your answer on the lines provided. Answer the questions **only** for the sections that are circled. Please do not mark your answers in the workbook.

The answers to the exercises are located in the back of the workbook.

1

MATH COMPUTATION Multiplication of Whole Numbers

1 (a) (b) (c) (d) (e)   5 (a) (b) (c) (d) (e)   9 _____

2 (a) (b) (c) (d) (e)   6 (a) (b) (c) (d) (e)   10 _____

3 (a) (b) (c) (d) (e)   7 (a) (b) (c) (d) (e)   11 _____

4 (a) (b) (c) (d) (e)   8 (a) (b) (c) (d) (e)   12 _____

MATH COMPUTATION Division of Whole Numbers

1 (a) (b) (c) (d) (e)   4 (a) (b) (c) (d) (e)   7 (a) (b) (c) (d) (e)   10 _____

2 (a) (b) (c) (d) (e)   5 (a) (b) (c) (d) (e)   8 (a) (b) (c) (d) (e)   11 _____

3 (a) (b) (c) (d) (e)   6 (a) (b) (c) (d) (e)   9 (a) (b) (c) (d) (e)   12 _____

MATH COMPUTATION Fractions

1 (a) (b) (c) (d) (e)   5 (a) (b) (c) (d) (e)   9 _____

2 (a) (b) (c) (d) (e)   6 (a) (b) (c) (d) (e)   10 _____

3 (a) (b) (c) (d) (e)   7 (a) (b) (c) (d) (e)   11 _____

4 (a) (b) (c) (d) (e)   8 (a) (b) (c) (d) (e)   12 _____

MATH COMPUTATION Decimals

1 (a) (b) (c) (d) (e)   5 (a) (b) (c) (d) (e)   9 _____

2 (a) (b) (c) (d) (e)   6 (a) (b) (c) (d) (e)   10 _____

3 (a) (b) (c) (d) (e)   7 (a) (b) (c) (d) (e)   11 _____

4 (a) (b) (c) (d) (e)   8 (a) (b) (c) (d) (e)   12 _____

2

MATH COMPUTATION Integers

1 ⓐ ⓑ ⓒ ⓓ ⓔ   5 ⓐ ⓑ ⓒ ⓓ ⓔ   9 _____

2 ⓐ ⓑ ⓒ ⓓ ⓔ   6 ⓐ ⓑ ⓒ ⓓ ⓔ   10 _____

3 ⓐ ⓑ ⓒ ⓓ ⓔ   7 ⓐ ⓑ ⓒ ⓓ ⓔ   11 _____

4 ⓐ ⓑ ⓒ ⓓ ⓔ   8 ⓐ ⓑ ⓒ ⓓ ⓔ   12 _____

MATH COMPUTATION Percents

1 ⓐ ⓑ ⓒ ⓓ ⓔ   5 ⓐ ⓑ ⓒ ⓓ ⓔ   9 ⓐ ⓑ ⓒ ⓓ ⓔ

2 ⓐ ⓑ ⓒ ⓓ ⓔ   6 ⓐ ⓑ ⓒ ⓓ ⓔ   10 _____

3 ⓐ ⓑ ⓒ ⓓ ⓔ   7 ⓐ ⓑ ⓒ ⓓ ⓔ   11 _____

4 ⓐ ⓑ ⓒ ⓓ ⓔ   8 ⓐ ⓑ ⓒ ⓓ ⓔ   12 _____

APPLIED MATHEMATICS Number and Number Operations

1 ⓐ ⓑ ⓒ ⓓ   9 ⓐ ⓑ ⓒ ⓓ   17 ⓐ ⓑ ⓒ ⓓ   25 _____

2 ⓐ ⓑ ⓒ ⓓ   10 ⓐ ⓑ ⓒ ⓓ   18 ⓐ ⓑ ⓒ ⓓ   26 _____

3 ⓐ ⓑ ⓒ ⓓ   11 ⓐ ⓑ ⓒ ⓓ   19 ⓐ ⓑ ⓒ ⓓ   27 _____

4 ⓐ ⓑ ⓒ ⓓ   12 ⓐ ⓑ ⓒ ⓓ   20 ⓐ ⓑ ⓒ ⓓ   28 _____

5 ⓐ ⓑ ⓒ ⓓ   13 ⓐ ⓑ ⓒ ⓓ   21 ⓐ ⓑ ⓒ ⓓ   29 _____

6 ⓐ ⓑ ⓒ ⓓ   14 ⓐ ⓑ ⓒ ⓓ   22 ⓐ ⓑ ⓒ ⓓ

7 ⓐ ⓑ ⓒ ⓓ   15 ⓐ ⓑ ⓒ ⓓ   23 ⓐ ⓑ ⓒ ⓓ

8 ⓐ ⓑ ⓒ ⓓ   16 ⓐ ⓑ ⓒ ⓓ   24 ⓐ ⓑ ⓒ ⓓ

3

APPLIED MATHEMATICS Computation in Context

1 (a) (b) (c) (d)   5 (a) (b) (c) (d)   9 (a) (b) (c) (d)   13 _____

2 (a) (b) (c) (d)   6 (a) (b) (c) (d)   10 (a) (b) (c) (d)   14 _____

3 (a) (b) (c) (d)   7 (a) (b) (c) (d)   11 (a) (b) (c) (d)   15 _____

4 (a) (b) (c) (d)   8 (a) (b) (c) (d)   12 _____   16 _____

APPLIED MATHEMATICS Estimation

1 (a) (b) (c) (d)   5 (a) (b) (c) (d)   9 (a) (b) (c) (d)   13 _____

2 (a) (b) (c) (d)   6 (a) (b) (c) (d)   10 (a) (b) (c) (d)   14 _____

3 (a) (b) (c) (d)   7 (a) (b) (c) (d)   11 (a) (b) (c) (d)   15 _____

4 (a) (b) (c) (d)   8 (a) (b) (c) (d)   12 (a) (b) (c) (d)   16 _____

APPLIED MATHEMATICS Measurement

1 (a) (b) (c) (d)   6 (a) (b) (c) (d)   11 (a) (b) (c) (d)   16 (a) (b) (c) (d)

2 (a) (b) (c) (d)   7 (a) (b) (c) (d)   12 (a) (b) (c) (d)   17 (a) (b) (c) (d)

3 (a) (b) (c) (d)   8 (a) (b) (c) (d)   13 (a) (b) (c) (d)   18 _____

4 (a) (b) (c) (d)   9 (a) (b) (c) (d)   14 (a) (b) (c) (d)   19 _____

5 (a) (b) (c) (d)   10 (a) (b) (c) (d)   15 (a) (b) (c) (d)

APPLIED MATHEMATICS   Geometry and Spatial Sense

1 (a) (b) (c) (d)   6 (a) (b) (c) (d)   11 (a) (b) (c) (d)   16 _____

2 (a) (b) (c) (d)   7 (a) (b) (c) (d)   12 (a) (b) (c) (d)   17 _____

3 (a) (b) (c) (d)   8 (a) (b) (c) (d)   13 (a) (b) (c) (d)   18 _____

4 (a) (b) (c) (d)   9 (a) (b) (c) (d)   14 _____   19 _____

5 (a) (b) (c) (d)   10 (a) (b) (c) (d)   15 _____

APPLIED MATHEMATICS   Data Analysis

1 (a) (b) (c) (d)   4 (a) (b) (c) (d)   7 (a) (b) (c) (d)   10 _____

2 (a) (b) (c) (d)   5 (a) (b) (c) (d)   8 (a) (b) (c) (d)   11 (a) (b) (c) (d)

3 (a) (b) (c) (d)   6 (a) (b) (c) (d)   9 _____   12 _____

APPLIED MATHEMATICS   Statistics and Probability

1 (a) (b) (c) (d)   8 (a) (b) (c) (d)   15 _____

2 (a) (b) (c) (d)   9 (a) (b) (c) (d)   16 _____

3 (a) (b) (c) (d)   10 (a) (b) (c) (d)   17 _____

4 (a) (b) (c) (d)   11 (a) (b) (c) (d)   18 _____

5 (a) (b) (c) (d)   12 (a) (b) (c) (d)   19 _____

6 (a) (b) (c) (d)   13 (a) (b) (c) (d)

7 (a) (b) (c) (d)   14 (a) (b) (c) (d)

APPLIED MATHEMATICS   Patterns, Functions, Algebra

1 (a) (b) (c) (d)   6 (a) (b) (c) (d)   11 (a) (b) (c) (d)   14 _____

2 (a) (b) (c) (d)   7 (a) (b) (c) (d)   12 (a) (b) (c) (d)   15 _____

3 (a) (b) (c) (d)   8 (a) (b) (c) (d)   13 (a) (b) (c) (d)   16 _____

4 (a) (b) (c) (d)   9 (a) (b) (c) (d)

5 (a) (b) (c) (d)   10 (a) (b) (c) (d)

APPLIED MATHEMATICS   Problem Solving and Reasoning

1 (a) (b) (c) (d)   6 (a) (b) (c) (d)   11 (a) (b) (c) (d)   14 _____

2 (a) (b) (c) (d)   7 (a) (b) (c) (d)   12 (a) (b) (c) (d)   15 _____

3 (a) (b) (c) (d)   8 (a) (b) (c) (d)   13 (a) (b) (c) (d)   16 _____

4 (a) (b) (c) (d)   9 (a) (b) (c) (d)   17 _____

5 (a) (b) (c) (d)   10 (a) (b) (c) (d)   18 _____